T0208591

The Exform

Verso Futures

The law of the innermost form of the essay is heresy.
– Theodor Adorno

Verso Futures is a series of essay-length philosophical and political interventions by both emerging and established writers and thinkers from around the world. Each title in the series addresses the outer limits of political and social possibility.

Also available in Verso Futures:

The Exform

Nicolas Bourriaud

Translated by Erik Butler

VERSO

London • New York

First published in the English language by Verso 2016
Translation © Erik Butler 2016
Originally published as *La Exforma* © Adriana Hidalgo Editora,
Buenos Aires, 2015

1 3 5 7 9 10 8 6 4 2

Verso
UK: 6 Meard Street, London W1F 0EG
US: 388 Atlantic Ave, Brooklyn, NY 11217
versobooks.com

Verso is the imprint of New Left Books

ISBN-13: 978-1-78478-380-8 (PB)
ISBN-13: 978-1-78478-379-2 (HB)
ISBN-13: 978-1-78478-381-5 (UK EBK)
ISBN-13: 978-1-78478-382-2 (US EBK)

Names: Bourriaud, Nicolas, author.
Title: The exform / Nicolas Bourriaud ; Translated by Erik Butler.
Description: Brooklyn, NY : Verso, 2016.
Identifiers: LCCN 2016002300 (print) | LCCN 2016008503 (ebook) | ISBN
   9781784783808 (paperback) | ISBN 9781784783792 (hardback) | ISBN
   9781784783822 (Ebook)
Subjects: LCSH: Art – Philosophy. | Ideology. |
BISAC: PHILOSOPHY / Political.
Classification: LCC N66 .B68 2016 (print) | LCC
N66 (ebook) | DDC 700.1 – dc23
LC record available at http://lccn.loc.gov/2016002300

Typeset in Sabon by Hewer Text UK Ltd, Edinburgh, Scotland
Printed in the United States

Contents

The Exform

Things and phenomena used to surround us. Today it seems they threaten us in ghostly form, as unruly scraps that refuse to go away or persist even after vanishing into the air. Some maintain that the solution would be to forge a new contract with the planet, inaugurating an era in which things, animals and human beings stand on an equal footing. Until then, we inhabit an overfull world, living in archives ready to burst, among more and more perishable products, junk food and bottlenecks. All the while, capitalism boldly dreams its dream of 'frictionless' exchange: a universe where commodities – beings and objects alike – circulate without encountering the slightest obstacle. Yet ours is also an epoch of squandered energy: nuclear waste that won't go away, hulking stockpiles of unused goods, and domino effects triggered by industrial emissions polluting the atmosphere and oceans.

The most striking image of refuse and discharge occurs in the economic sphere: *junk bonds* with *toxic assets*; it's as if dangerous materials buried away in the balance sheets of obscure subsidiaries and mutualized portfolios had invaded the financial universe. The matter plainly reveals the *real* of globalism: a world haunted by the spectre of what is unproductive or unprofitable, waging war against all that is not already *at work* or in the process of becoming so. We have witnessed the realm of waste assume vast dimensions. Now it encompasses whatever resists assimilation – the banished, the unusable and the useless ... Waste, according to the dictionary, refers to *what is cast off when something is made*. The proletariat – the social class that capital has at its full disposal – is no longer found only in factories. It runs through the whole of the social body and comprises a people of the *abandoned*; its emblematic figures are the immigrant, the illegal and the homeless. Once upon a time, 'proletarian' referred to a worker who had been dispossessed of his labour. Our age has expanded the definition; it now includes all who have been stripped of experience (whatever it might be) and forced to replace *being* with *having* in their everyday lives. The delocalization of industrial production, massive 'downsizing', mounting political disregard for social welfare, as well as increasingly harsh immigration laws, have led to the emergence of grey zones where surplus human beings vegetate – whether as undocumented workers or as the chronically unemployed. At the same time, an 'economy of impurity' exists in plain view: people who process fish, clean buildings, move houses, and dispose of diseased livestock – social categories covered by the caste of 'untouchables' in India.

It would appear that the 'spectral dance' Marx describes in *Capital* has assumed a new form today. This book proposes to analyze, by way of the optical machinery afforded by contemporary art, the effects of this mutation on our modes of thinking and feeling.

One catches sight of the characteristic dance of a given epoch through relations between art and politics. Since the beginning of the nineteenth century, both spheres have been fashioned by the *centrifugal* force created by the Industrial Revolution: on one hand, a movement of social exclusion; on the other, the categorical rejection of certain signs, objects and images. Here, the model of thermodynamics holds. Social energy produces waste; it generates zones of exclusion where the proletariat, popular culture, the squalid and the immoral pile up in a jumble – the devalued ensemble of *what one cannot bear to see*. The 'spectral dance', in other words, is the *phantasmagoria* specific to an epoch. It follows from the orchestration of regulated exchanges between centre and periphery – the organization governing what is official and what is rejected, what is dominant and what is dominated – which make the borders between realms into the dynamic site fuelling History. From the nineteenth century on, the political and artistic avant-gardes have made it their task to help the excluded accede to power, whether by stealth or in plain view – that is, to reverse the thermodynamic machine, to capitalize on what capital has repressed, to recycle putative *waste* and make it a source of energy. In the process, centrifugal movement is supposed to change course, bring the proletariat back to the centre, restore the dropout to culture, and introduce what has been demeaned into works of art. But now, two centuries later, does this dynamic still produce any energy?

Ideology, psychoanalysis and art represent the principal fields of battle for *realist thinking*; in their respective domains, Marx, Freud and Courbet laid the foundations. All three refuted the hierarchies their society advanced in the name of its *Ideal*, questioned the presuppositions underlying its mechanisms of exclusion, and sought procedures for *unveiling* them. Today, this realist strategy seems best suited for founding a political theory of art capable of moving beyond what is merely 'politically correct' and simple denunciations of mechanisms of authority or repression. Accordingly, what is qualified as *realist* in the following is art that resists this operation of triage; likewise, *realist* describes works that lift the ideological veils which apparatuses of power drape over the mechanism of expulsion and its refuse, whether material or not.

This is the realm the *exformal*: the site where border negotiations unfold between what is rejected and what is admitted, products and waste. *Exform* designates a point of contact, a 'socket' or 'plug', in the process of exclusion and inclusion – a sign that switches between centre and periphery, floating between dissidence and power.

Gestures of expulsion and the waste it entails, the point where the *exform* emerges, constitute an authentically organic link between the aesthetic and the political. Their parallel evolution over the last two centuries may be summarized as a series of inclusive and exclusive movements: on the one hand, the ever-renewed separation of the significant from the *insignificant* in art; on the other, the ideological frontiers drawn by biopolitics – the governance of human bodies – at the heart of a given society. Since the beginning of modernity – at least since Gustave Courbet, although one could go back to Caravaggio – motifs of the depreciated and devalued have constituted the primal and privileged matter in works of art: bundles of asparagus or ladies of easy virtue appear and outrage grand paintings of History; this is the famous 'end of eloquence' (flowery, nineteenth-century elegance), whose death throes Georges Bataille described apropos of Manet. In the political sphere, rejection yields the class of the excluded: the proletariat – a term that referred, in Roman antiquity, to those whose only wealth was their children (*proles*). Today, the proletarian seems to stand at a great remove from the status Marx granted him as the *subject of History*. Even in the collective imaginary, the illegal immigrant has taken his place. In turn, psychoanalysis developed the concept of *repression* – the operation through which the subject evacuates, into the unconscious, all representations it cannot reconcile with the ego ideal. Exclusion from the *polis*, repression outside the realm of consciousness, and the *devalued* matter that the artist takes up attest to the presence of a mechanism of expulsion.

What does progressive politics mean if not the taking-into-account of the excluded? What is a psychoanalyst if not a practitioner whose field is the repressed? Finally, what is an artist if not someone who deems that anything at all – including the foulest refuse – is capable of acquiring aesthetic value? All that is hidden, evacuated or banished derives from this centrifugal logic, which consigns beings and things to the world of *waste* and holds them there in the name of the Ideal. And so, figures of exclusion traverse the unconscious, ideology, art and History. They constitute a filigraned motif linking together the 'ragpicker of History' described by Walter Benjamin, Bataille's *heterology*, Althusser's theses on ideology, the programme of *cultural studies*, and materialist thinking in contemporary art.

That said, it would be simplistic to content oneself with protesting rejection in the name of egalitarianism; nor is it enough to recuperate filth in order to be a great artist. The absolute uniformity arising from a world that had banished all separation – a landscape of infinite storehouses where nothing is discarded – would soon turn into a nightmare. Denouncing the process of triage *per se* means promoting idealism in reverse. Materialism is not the reversal or the inversion of idealist discourse. It does not propose centrifugal motion as the remedy for centripetal motion; instead, it substitutes the movement of a generalized *decentring* for both: the disorientation of compasses, now stripped of their normative 'magnetic north' . . .

To write this book, I *began with a vague idea and confronted it with clear images*: in Jean-Luc Godard's *La Chinoise*, this watchword sprawls across the apartment wall of a group of students miming Mao's cultural revolution. Instead of offering an account of contemporary artistic practice in order to deduce a theory, as in previous works, the book at hand steers the opposite course. If invoking Benjamin and Bataille represents something familiar to readers, the prominent place granted to Louis Althusser – a singular figure in twentieth-century thought – may come as a surprise. Yet if one seeks to problematize relations between aesthetics and politics, form and theory, and ideology and praxis, engagement with Althusser's writings proves inescapable. Moreover, when evaluating the positions of Jacques Rancière, Alain Badiou or Slavoj Žižek, it is necessary to refer to the man who taught the first two and exercised a decisive influence on the third (Žižek's doctoral adviser – and later, analyst – was Jacques-Alain Miller, who also studied under Althusser). That said, if his thought echoes in their works, one cannot fail to note that they hardly signal as much.

Why is Althusser, this 'philosophers' philosopher', quoted so little in contemporary theoretical debates? To begin with, most of his students broke with the path charted in May 1968. In *Althusser's Lesson*, which appeared in 1973, Rancière denounced his teacher's archaic Stalinism; in her study of Antonio Gramsci, Chantal Mouffe set out to find the fresh air she deemed lacking in Althusser's confining dogmatism; others, such as Jacques-Alain Miller and Jean-Claude Milner, simply left for the Lacanian camp. Secondly, Althusser was an apparatchik of the French Communist Party and a notorious psychotic, institutionalized on many occasions; he wound up killing his partner, Hélène Rytman, before vanishing under an immense cloak of silence. In other words, he hardly meets the requirements of the contemporary jet set of philosophy. In more than one way, then, Althusser is an *embarrassing* figure, an elephant in the plush lounge of contemporary thought. It is a riddle for the ages how this pachyderm managed to unite such rigour of thought and clarity of exposition (occasionally didactic *ad nauseam*) with the manic-depressive psychosis that bedevilled him.

Notwithstanding the resurgence of Marxism – which was augmented when the semblance of financial propriety collapsed in autumn 2008, during the crisis of so-called subprime lending – what interest does Althusser hold today? For one, his writings are far from obsolete; historical context has charged them with new significance. The texts written during the philosopher's years of public silence (1980–90), especially the remarkable 'Underground Current of the Materialism of the Encounter' and *Sur la philosophie* – as well as other posthumous (or semi-posthumous) publications such as his course on Machiavelli and *Writings on Psychoanalysis*, to say nothing of typewritten texts he shared with friends – present Althusser in a wholly different light than the one suggested by the last pamphlet to appear before the 'drama': the off-putting *Ce qui ne peut plus durer dans le parti communiste* (*What Can No Longer Stand in the Communist Party*). Althusser's philosophy offers a surprising web of connections between Marxism of the most scientific stripe and a strange obsession with emptiness, chaos, the carnivalesque and imposture; still more, it presents an unsettlingly dreamlike vision of ideology. These aspects lend his work a singular intensity at a time when philosophy and art have made fashionable a form of Marxism that proves all the more radical for no longer occupying a position on the chessboard of global politics – Marxism all the purer, that is, because it waves stumps where it once had hands. Rereading Althusser in light of twenty-first-century cultural debates allows us to see the complex relations between art and politics with fresh eyes and discern what escapes the naïve formulations to which they are so often reduced.

My generation awakened to intellectual life in the 1980s. I discovered Althusser through his posthumous writings. Initially, my view was just as unfavourable as it was poorly documented: Althusser seemed to be a dogmatic bureaucrat, a vestige of the Brezhnev era. In contrast, Gilles Deleuze and Félix Guattari, Michel Foucault, Roland Barthes, Jean Baudrillard, Jean-François Lyotard and Jacques Lacan immediately struck me – and my peers – as contemporaries who furnished conceptual tools for decoding our own times. What could interminable exegeses of Marx have to offer compared to *A Thousand Plateaus* or *Discipline and Punish*? Such studies seemed to have been written by a philosopher at odds with events – a hardcore structuralist in the age of postmodernism, a strictly observant Leninist during *perestroika*. *La pensée Althusser*, as it was known in the philosopher's glory days, had been relegated to the attic of history, along with Afghan coats, bell-bottom pants and Jefferson Airplane records ... In a word, Althusser – the official representative of a gigantic continent in the course of sinking – had become completely inaudible by the mid-1980s.

This held all the more because a passion for the *minor*, continuing the 'counterculture' of the 1960s and 1970s at another frequency, gripped my generation. Postcolonial theory and cultural studies, while still in their infancy, were largely prepared by lateral moves away from 'official' culture – what has come to be called *mainstream*. Yet in theorizing 'minor literature', Deleuze and Guattari initiated a quest for singularities and insularities that was clearly incompatible with the land masses of intellectual history, including orthodox Marxism. Our natural milieu was the cultural underground; our aesthetic breviary consisted of obscure fin-de-siècle authors and the outsiders of art history. In relatively systematic fashion, we went looking for dissident writers, philosophers pushed off the high roads of intellectual history, and cultural mavericks. We granted priority to what the immense Marxist and modernist continent had crushed. We made pilgrimages to Trieste, Lisbon, Prague or Buenos Aires, which had become

literary capitals *par excellence*. Individuals were redis-
covered whose eccentricity had held them distant from
manifestos and programmes: Fernando Pessoa, Jorge
Luis Borges, Eva Hesse or Gordon Matta-Clark – thinkers too subtle, or irredentist, for the radical collectivism
of the twentieth century.

To appreciate the nature of the intellectual moment, it
warrants mention that the modernist debacle left behind
a landscape in tatters. For anyone young in the 1980s,
nothing seemed more exhilarating than the 'weak thought'
advocated by Gianni Vattimo, Baudrillard's 'simulacra'
or Paul Virilio's *Aesthetics of Disappearance*. Nothing
could be more productive than to move what had been
derived from the vertical dimension of History onto the
geographical plane of a pure present. Global suspicion
towards the theories and manifestos of the preceding
decades collided headlong with 'classical' Marxism. It
reached its climax in 1989, when the Iron Curtain
collapsed on the short twentieth century' and inaugurated
the era of globalization.

At the time, we failed to recognize that the seductive
motif of *minority* – that is, the principle of pulverization
it introduced to philosophy, the points opening onto
dissident narratives that had been kept in the shadows –
camouflaged a demolition enterprise much larger in
scope. What we had viewed as the melting of the ideological ice caps, the rupture of continental plates restricting
thought, actually covered up – and quite discreetly – a
process of political liquidation: the ensuing flood carried
off multiple blocks of resistance, and their disappearance
facilitated progressive amnesia, resignation and power-
lessness. When class struggle gave way to localized struggles and engagement, when the notorious *reality principle*

took the place of economic utopia, when the avant-garde vanished in a cloud of synchronous propositions, we were left with no choice but to start from scratch. This book seeks to participate in this new beginning – even as it refuses to *return* to anything at all.

I

The Proletarian Unconscious

The Drama at the Hotel PLM Saint-Jacques

On 15 March 1980, more than 300 members of the *École Freudienne de Psychanalyse* gather at the PLM Saint-Jacques, a hotel in the fifteenth arrondissement of Paris. The hour is grave: in a missive dated 5 January, Jacques Lacan summoned the faithful to tell them why he has decided to dissolve the school. For some time now, rumours have been circulating that his capacities are diminished – that he is senile, over and done. Obsessed with devising a topology of the unconscious, Lacan has been confusing the participants in his seminar by tracing geometrical figures on the blackboard and using pieces of string to make Moebius strips and *tori*. News that the organization founded sixteen years earlier is now being dismantled hits the disciples hard. Some of them feel abandoned; others consider it the epilogue to an intellectual collapse.

The venerable master is seated behind an ordinary table facing two rows of chairs; there is no platform in the room. He has already been speaking for a while, in a very low voice, when someone comes to the door. The young woman 'screening' visitors asks the new arrival if he has been invited. The stranger responds that yes, absolutely, he was invited: 'by the Holy Ghost, and not by God the Father, but that's even better'. The attendees hear the door open noisily, and the whole room murmurs. Everyone realizes who has forced his way in. Among the participants, Jacques-Alain Miller – Lacan's son-in-law and spiritual kinsman – is sitting in the first row on the left, next to an empty chair. Suddenly, he recalls,

> I feel something like a breeze; someone has just rushed to my side. I turn, it's Althusser. I haven't seen him in years. We speak to each other. He is in a state of agitation I have never seen him in. I suggest that he go with me to the rear of the room, listen to his comments, try to calm him. He gets up and takes the floor.[1]

Althusser lights his pipe, moves towards where a podium should be, and shakes Lacan's hand – even though Lacan does not recognize him right away. 'I showed all the respect I felt towards this great old man, who was dressed like a pierrot in a blue-checked tweed jacket.'[2] Seizing the microphone, the philosopher calls those in attendance fearful and cowardly, strangely comparing them to 'a woman attempting to sift our lentils while war is

---

1 Jacques-Alain Miller, conversation with Olivier Corpet and François Matheron, in Louis Althusser, *Writings on Psychoanalysis: Freud and Lacan*, trans. Jeffrey Mehlman (New York: Columbia University Press, 1999), 181.

2 Louis Althusser, *The Future Lasts Forever: A Memoir*, trans. Richard Veasey (New York: The New Press, 1995), 188.

breaking out'.[3] He declares that he is speaking 'on behalf of . . . the worldwide crowd of analysands, millions of men, women, and children', in order that 'their existence and . . . problems and the risks they run when they enter into analysis be taken seriously'.[4] 'That's it, that's just it', Lacan is supposed to have agreed . . .

Althusser is escorted to the door.

The spectacular episode at the PLM Saint-Jacques, which occurred six months before Althusser killed his partner and disappeared from public life forever, has long counted as a matter belonging to his medical file – a sign foreshadowing the tragedy. Before long, Roland Barthes and Jean-Paul Sartre died (on 26 March and 15 April 1980, respectively). In September the following year, Lacan passed away, and Althusser's words remained a dead letter. Why had he staged this intervention? What was the point of bursting onto the psychoanalytic scene and making the 'analysed' heard, loud and clear? Apropos of the Lacanian school being disbanded, a brief and hastily written text – which remained unpublished during Althusser's lifetime – describes his point of view:

On that I have no opinion, but it is a political act, and such an act is not taken alone, as Lacan did, but should be reflected on and discussed democratically by all the interested parties, in the first rank of which are your 'masses', who are the analysands, your 'masses' and

3 Elisabeth Roudinesco, *Jacques Lacan & Co.: A History of Psychoanalysis in France, 1925–1985*, trans. Jeffrey Mehlman (Chicago: University of Chicago Press, 1990), 659.

4 Althusser, *Writings on Psychoanalysis*, 137–8.

your 'real teachers' which the analysands are . . . otherwise, it's despotism, even if it's enlightened.[5]

In other words, Althusser took the floor in the name of democracy – in the name of the anonymous proletariat formed, in his eyes, by the 'mass' of patients. The theorist of 'class struggle in philosophy' shifted his discourse to the couch in order to equate material production and the human psyche; he described the process of the analytic cure in ouvrierist accents, evoking 'the analysands, of which there are perhaps millions in the world', as a new class fighting for its rights. Althusser continues:

> then there's the price they have to pay (I'm not even speaking of the money they have to fork out) as much to accomplish their own work as analysands (the often atrocious and always very difficult and testing '*Durcharbeiten*,' at the edge of abysses, often on the brink of suicide) . . .[6]

Such words generally apply to factory work. *Durcharbeiten*, a Freudian concept translated as 'working-through' (*perlaboration* in French), refers to repetitive labour: in analysis, working-through means returning to the same scenes until repression disappears and the patient achieves conscious knowledge of the history of his or her symptom.

Does this mean that the psychoanalyst is a kind of foreman supervising the ungrateful and mechanical labour of his subordinates? Was Althusser pointing to a new form of alienation, or to a particular instance of general alienation? The philosopher makes his position

5 Ibid., 132.
6 Ibid., 142.

clear in a series of allusions. He criticizes the division of labour in analysis: 'sessions without preestablished length, without a contract determining length, as if the analyst were alone able to impose his own measure of length', which prompts the question: 'why wouldn't it be the analysand, if that is how one is reasoning, who would impose his own?'[7] 'Measure of length' represents the nodal point for Marxist reflections on labour. Ever since Frederick Winslow Taylor's theses on the rationalization and chronometry of factory work (1893) – which echo Benjamin Franklin's famous axiom ('time is money') – mastery of time has been fused with social activity: hyperspecialization and management of both work and 'leisure' represent the principal factors of alienation. For Althusser, the analysand can only liken himself to an intellectual proletarian. *The wretched of the earth* are also found on couches . . .

This amounts to the thesis advanced in *Anti-Oedipus*: the unconscious is not a miniature theatre, but an immense factory: a production site filled with 'desiring machines' that flow less into domestic and familial space than into social space and metaphysical lines of flight. That said, it is doubtful that Lacan – against whom Deleuze and Guattari's book takes direct aim – ever considered the unconscious a 'theatre', or that the Oedipus complex ever obscured his view. The war-machine of *Anti-Oedipus* – which appeared in 1972 to combat a Freudian psychoanalysis still under the spell of parental relations – underestimated what Lacan could contribute to the cause. In fact, the Lacanian unconscious does not function as a familial drama at all; it works through channels that only

7   Ibid.

topology can describe. If one discounts the lexical and thematic differences, Lacan could only have agreed with Deleuze and Guattari when they affirmed that psychoanalysis does not seek to unearth tawdry secrets, but to set chains of signification in motion – the 'desiring machines' of *Anti-Oedipus*. All the same, a profound difference holds on the matter of desire: Lacan is much more Spinozan than he appears at first glance.

Anti-Oedipus brought a political opposition of the times to the fore. Like Althusser, Deleuze and Guattari presented a *leftist* critique of psychoanalysis, attacking Lacan on the plane of ideology. They went after the same Lacan who had struck out at students of the University of Vincennes – not long after May 1968 – when he declared that the revolutionaries wanted another 'master'. 'And you'll get one', he added. Indeed, Lacan's lifestyle and the haughty scepticism oozing from his discourse were less revolutionary than his thinking. The correspondences between Deleuze and Guattari's metaphors of industrialization and the class struggle that Althusser brought into the psychoanalytic field are striking. These three thinkers describe the unconscious as the natural extension of political combat. They go to battle under the banner of a critique of productivism – in the name of a proletariat of the unconscious with as little self-awareness as the subjects of ideology.

At the time, this debate might have appeared technical, restricted to psychoanalysis or philosophy. Since then, however, it has proven of capital importance to parties who have made it their own and displaced it onto another site, where other relations are articulated between politics and mental production: the realm of art. The question of whether the unconscious is a factory or a theatre involves asking about the nature of what it produces, and how it does so. Does it produce spectacles, revelations, or, rather, arrangements of 'particles' (as Deleuze and Guattari put it)? The distinction is crucial. Since the 1960s – from minimalist and conceptual art up to Mike Kelley and Pierre Huyghe – the individual work has been measured in terms of general production: its formats of visibility and social conditions, whether spatial or temporal. In other words, reflection on the *norm* represents the point of departure. It's as if art had set out to pursue and perpetuate the founding concern of 'French theory': to shed light on norms and what remains *unthought*, by analyzing the social and biopolitical conditions for our utterances and behaviours.

Now, in the early twenty-first century, artistic production directly descends from Althusser's mortal battle with idealism: to demonstrate, in an unremitting and occasionally violent way, the absolute materiality of the void, chance, ideology and the unconscious – that is, everything constituting the natural preserve of the ineffable or mystical. Contemporary art proceeds with a similar anti-idealism, which finds expression in its will to concretize economic abstractions, represent immaterial fluxes, produce chance artificially, and lend form to the invisible (or to certain spiritual forces). Contemporary art's motto, 'Everything admits figuration' – that is, even what is impalpable counts as raw material or surface – echoes Althusser's declaration that 'everything is material'. Inasmuch as artists devote equal attention to preparing, making and exhibiting their works, one also senses the dream of *activity without waste*: a process brought out into the open, whereby everything is useful or significant. This, incidentally, is not unrelated to the aims of the psychoanalytic cure. What, exactly, does an idea, sensation or sign produce in terms of the circuit of distribution it occupies and the format it assumes? In what way is artistic form overdetermined (to employ an Althusserian term) by the discourses surrounding it?

If art were a machine, it would be a kind of *eidetic generator*: attitudes, gestures, scenarios, discussions and human relations – the vaguest and most unsayable matters – can take shape here. The common denominator of the varied activities comprising the field of art is *formalization*. Translating an idea, a sensation, into organization and order gives it new meaning. Now, the unconscious – which (unbeknownst to us) gives concrete form to our obsessions and the traumas of daily life – offers the artistic tool of choice: an operative model, a representative *exform*. In other words, the art of our day is wholly inscribed in an ongoing debate about the metaphor used to describe the unconscious – Deleuze and Guattari's quarrel with Freudian psychoanalysis. Is the unconscious a theatre or a factory? Guattari was the fiercest critic of frozen clinical dogma and inert chemistry: he called for psychoanalysis to discard the 'invisible lab coats' that kept it from questioning itself, and to start over on the basis of artistic creation. 'More so', he wrote, 'given that the domain of psychiatry has established itself as the extension of, and at the interface with, aesthetic domains'.[8]

Psychoanalysis aims to 'produce' human beings who are fully alive, just as a factory manufactures material goods. One question remains, however: what can be produced without any waste? Althusser asks what the

8   Félix Guattari, *The Three Ecologies*, trans. Ian Pindar and Paul Sutton (London: Bloomsbury, 2008), 39.

object of psychoanalysis is, then gives an answer by describing a bloody epic. The analytic cure involves 'the effects, prolonged in the surviving adult, of the extraordinary adventure that, from birth to the liquidation of the Oedipus complex, transforms a small animal engendered by a man and a woman into a little human child'.[9] Once we have become adults, a state of amnesia about this 'battle' prevails: 'the wounds, infirmities, . . . aches'[10] and cruel 'training' it implies. Self-production cannot occur without something *breaking* . . .

Louis Althusser Reread by Philip K. Dick

When Althusser's death was announced on 22 October 1990, my first reaction was surprise that he had still been alive, such a heavy cloud of oblivion had descended on him. Then, *The Future Lasts Forever* appeared. This posthumous text, published in 1992, was written between March and June 1985 – five years after events. Here, Althusser seeks to justify the dismissal that occurred after he murdered his partner in the apartment at the École Normale Supérieure he had occupied for more than twenty years. Found 'not responsible for his actions', he was interned at the Sainte-Anne Hospital as an emergency measure. Thanks to the intervention of former pupils, he escaped judgement. Althusser was the object of psychiatric attention for three years, and then relegated to what Foucault called 'the life of infamous men' – a silence that could be measured only in terms of

9   Althusser, *Writings on Psychoanalysis*, 22.
10   Ibid.

his erstwhile glory. There is no point in detailing the saga Althusser describes in his autobiography. It suffices to identify the key elements. His mother, whose 'purity' he idealizes, was engaged to a young man named Louis, who fell during the First World War; she married his brother, and from this union a son was born who inherited the departed uncle's name. In due course, Althusser describes his years of captivity in a German prison camp, which nourished his reclusive nature; his shift from Catholicism to communism; his defloration, at the age of twenty-nine, by a woman older than himself (with whom he lived until he took her life); and, finally, his teaching position in Paris at the École Normale Supérieure, where his students included Jacques Derrida, Michel Foucault, Jacques Rancière, Jacques-Alain Miller, Alain Badiou, Régis Debray, Étienne Balibar, Robert Linhart, Chantal Mouffe and Clément Rosset. The whole of his story is punctuated by recurrent manic-depressive crises.

To my knowledge, no other philosophical autobiography like this one exists. Throughout this *fascinating* text – in the literal sense – the author weaves in interpretations resembling so many aspects of an analytic cure *a posteriori* that started forty years earlier, in 1947. The book teems with incongruous ideas and parentheses that never close; the author's need for precision prompts pullulating associations: high-flown philosophical discourse shot through with slang and vernacular cheek, implacable logic swollen with tumorous delirium. Occasionally, the style becomes totally unhinged. For all that, the tension leading both author and reader to the *dénouement* never slackens: the motivating drama – the murder Althusser seeks to explicate by summoning all the circumstances of his past life – draws a singular line of division between the biographical and theoretical domains. An initial reading yields a psychoanalytic account closely resembling the unbridled discourse of an analysand on the couch. At the same time, one cannot help but think of the Joycean *stream of consciousness* – or the final texts of Antonin Artaud – more than the model Althusser himself invokes: Jean-Jacques Rousseau's *Confessions*. Over and above a biography with its specific *mise-en-scène*, one reads a philosopher revisiting his entire oeuvre – and, with it, Marxism – from a wholly original perspective: that of 'aleatory materialism', presented here for the first time.[11]

In effect, Althusser conceived this delirious book according to an exacting theoretical principle that resumes a long-term line of psychoanalytic and philosophical questioning. 'I consider as fundamentally religious', he had written in 1966, 'the concepts of *origin* and *genesis* . . . when taken, of course, in the rigorous sense constituted by their *couple*.'[12] In contrast to the notion of *genesis*, which presupposes that the mature individual has been programmed '*from the origin* of the . . . process of engendering', here, Althusser writes his itinerary from a standpoint within philosophy AND madness. The view does not come from an indifferent point of origin whose evolution must simply be unfolded. Instead, it follows the logic of emergence, eruption or springing-up (*surgissement*), whereby 'something *new* begins to *function in an autonomous manner*'.[13] This logic of emergence – as opposed to the logic of an origin – points back to the

---

11 Ibid.
12 Ibid., 41.
13 Ibid., 42.

analytic cure: nothing preconditions what *emerges* in the course of the narrative, and nothing else comes in to explain it. As such, Althusser's story represents a series of 'absolute beginnings starting from nothing'. *The Future Lasts Forever* functions according to the principle of aleatory materialism: it starts from the void and proceeds according to the rules of chaos, progressing in concentric circles that arise from the collision of facts, ideas, buckled analyses, and digressions which shake, in every sense, the traditional conception of the *memoir*.

Strictly speaking, the unconscious has nothing to do with memory for Althusser: 'If we say that the unconscious is a memory, we lapse back into one of the worst concepts of psychology(!), and we are tempted to think that memory = history, that therapy = rectified rememoration = correct historicity . . .'[14] In other words, 'the unconscious is no more a memory than is absolutely any functioning mechanism, including the most advanced cybernetic mechanisms. On that, if my "memory" is correct, there are some rather good things in Lacan.'[15] It bears repeating: for Althusser, origin and genesis are religious and idealist notions – 'the concept of memory *takes the place of*, *represents* the equivalent of, a *genesis*'.[16] The primary material presented in *The Future Lasts Forever* is not memory as, say, Proust understood it, but anamnesis such as it surges up in the psychoanalytic cure. Accordingly, this book of falsified memories owes nothing to classic rememoration, nor to the logical order the latter imposes. For Althusser, 'the structure of every

14 Ibid., 44.
15 Ibid., 45.
16 Ibid., 46.

genesis is necessarily teleological'. That is, one can find in (supposed) origins only what one seeks in the present: 'every process is *governed by its end*'.[17] Here, too, the present modifies the past, and not vice versa.

Instead of *births*, Althusser seeks unforeseen and stupefying *eruptions*. Autobiography becomes a kind of science fiction. Philip K. Dick might have dreamed up these *memoirs without memory, without genesis or origin*. More than a philosopher's account of his life, *replicants* with mnemonic implants come to mind – as do the vertiginous temporalities that provide the framework for novels such as *Ubik* and *The Man in the High Castle*. This conception of temporality extending from the future to the past – where the origin amounts to either a lure or an agent of chaos – evokes Dick's theories, according to which the commonplace understanding of History is only a fiction, and the world we inhabit just one version of reality among others.

Even though Althusser's narrative is the confession of a murderer enlisting all the arguments at his disposal to make the reader understand the reasons for the 'drama' in which his life culminated – and then pardon him – an implacable clinical tableau doubles it. One element in particular warrants attention. At the end of the book, in chapter XXIII, when Althusser seems to have exhausted all his rhetorical tricks, a singular character takes the stage: an 'old doctor friend' appears, reviews the facts, and offers conclusions of his own. This party remarks 'an extraordinary set of events some of which were purely accidental, others not'; at any rate, 'the whole

17 Ibid., 57.

configuration could in no way have been foreseen'.[18] A doctor? Needless to say, such a figure signifies authorized, scientific opinion. In all likelihood, this 'old doctor friend' never existed.[19] Here, too, the reader is drawn into a strange screenplay . . .

Bryan Singer's *The Usual Suspects* comes to mind. The film tells the story in a long flashback. The disabled protagonist – the only one to escape the explosion that concludes the story – is being interrogated by a police inspector. Played by Kevin Spacey, the protagonist-narrator recounts the events he witnessed and presents himself as the plaything of circumstances orchestrated by a mysterious and terrifying gangster, a certain 'Keyzer Söze'. As the film draws to a close and the suspect is released – having delivered an account that seems to clear him – the inspector looks around his office; he realizes that more or less all the names the suspect has mentioned surround him: on the poster pinned up behind him, a coffee mug, a mat on the desk . . . The crafty witness has used all the signifiers at hand to devise a plausible story without any connection to the actual facts. In the final sequence, we see him limping down the street; his step gradually becomes steadier until he reaches a limousine and a chauffeur opens the door. We understand that the man pretending to be crippled is none other than Keyzer Söze himself – whatever his 'true' identity may be. This could well be the point of Althusser's confession: to requisition all available signifiers – from Marxism to

---

18   Eric Marty, *Louis Althusser, un sujet sans procés. Autonomie d'un passé très récent* (Paris: Gallimard, 1999), 273. (Althusser, *The Future*, 280.)

19   Marty, *Louis Althusser*, 42.

psychoanalysis, from Spinoza to Derrida – in order to concoct a plea before the tribunal of History; acquitted, he would leave his invalid condition behind and stride down the high road of philosophy.

How did relations between 'unreason' and culture evolve from the 1960s on? Significantly, two of the great French *maîtres à penser*, Jacques Lacan and Louis Althusser, were frequently described as mad. The latter, of course, presented a few guarantees: he was literally psychotic. Lacan, on the other hand, was a professional psychoanalyst. But that did not keep the media then – just as it doesn't prevent conservative intellectuals now – from speaking of him as an eccentric guru and a megalomaniac. There are thousands of rumours about the founder of the École Freudienne: his habit of pulling wads of bills out of his office desk, his compulsive behaviour, odd attire, and obstinate refusal to stop for red lights, etc. Althusser, for his part, has come right out and told us that he was a kleptomaniac, that he tried to steal a nuclear submarine from the Toulon harbour, and that he staged a 'first-rate non-violent hold-up in the Bank of Paris and the Netherlands'.[20] Mao Zedong wanted to meet him, he claims; he also sent letters to the president of the United States and demanded an audience with the pope. What warrants our attention is not the relationship between thought and 'madness' in general, but a more specific question: how to think *with* madness. How does theoretical discourse negotiate with nervous illness? The question is acute in Althusser's case, and proves all the more insistent because he never resolved the matter. Instead, he attempted to address the issue within a singular

20 Althusser, *The Future*, 349.

dispositive; the combination of psychoanalytic concepts and philosophy (the 'symptomatic reading' he applied to Marx) with his abiding claim to being an analysand produced unprecedented effects.

A third personage is also necessary for understanding the philosophical scene: Michel Foucault. In 1946, shortly before Althusser took up his teaching duties, the two met at the École Normale Supérieure. At the time, Foucault's peers believed that 'his psychological balance was, to say the least, fragile': 'one day, someone teaching at the ENS found him lying on the floor of a room where he had just sliced up his chest with a razor'.[21] There can be no doubt that such borderline behaviour stemmed from Foucault's experience of shame and pain in being homosexual – as, alas, was often the case in France at the time. All the same, 'when *Histoire de la folie* came out, everyone who knew him saw immediately that it was connected to his personal history'.[22] But if Foucault constantly skirted madness, he managed to escape it – unlike Althusser. Their friendship weathered a few storms, which stemmed from Foucault's vigorous criticism of Marxism, starting with *The Order of Things*. All the same, it lasted until Foucault's death in 1984. Ultimately, both thinkers trained their philosophical weapons at the same adversary: subjugation. The 'ideological state apparatuses' Althusser analyzed include the hospital and the prison. The institutional critiques Foucault pursued – although less 'massive' and more focused on the dispositives through which knowledge and power are articulated

21 Didier Eribon, *Foucault*, trans. Betsy Wing (Cambridge: Harvard University Press, 1991), 26.
22 Ibid., 27.

– concern how certain discourses are filtered, excluded and discredited, which is what Althusser's writings do too.

Althusser refers to Foucault frequently when evoking his psychiatric woes. On the one hand, he does so because of the nature of his friend's works: Althusser had hailed *Histoire de la folie* with genuine philosophical enthusiasm. What is more, Foucault's publication of the confessions of Pierre Rivière – a case of parricidal dementia – appears to have provided an (unacknowledged) model for *The Future Lasts Forever*. 'I am neither alive nor dead and, though I have not been buried', Althusser writes, 'I am "bodiless". I am simply *missing*, which was Foucault's splendid definition of madness.'[23] At the end of his life, Althusser considered himself to number among the 'missing'; claiming that he was now 'bodiless', he could finally assume his *disguise (imposture)*. By his own account, he had hardly read Marx and knew only a few passages from Spinoza. Over the course of his autobiography, Althusser takes the stage as an ingenious usurper, cannily elaborating philosophical concepts based on whatever spare excerpts happen to lie within reach.

Announcing his own *bricolage* and *non-savoir*, Althusser in fact enunciates the fundamental imposture of philosophy in general: upon reflection, all discourse signals its alienated condition; for him, this alienation has assumed the specific traits of madness. An ingenious forger, Althusser even attributes an array of hilarious false quotes to his psychoanalyst René Diatkine, which introduce 'Transference and Countertransference'. Althusserian thinking, to employ Eric Marty's apt phrase, qualifies as

---

23 Althusser, *The Future*, 23.

'carnivalesque'. It pronounces the absolute singularity of the event in the madman's discourse, an eruption troubling borders and systems. Its point of departure lies in the 'great confinement' Foucault described as the ideological signature of the classical age: the separation of Madness and Reason, the inauguration of an 'inside' and an 'outside'. Nor should one forget that this point – more precisely, the Cartesian *cogito* – is precisely where Jacques Derrida begins his withering critique of Foucault: thought, even if it is mad, founds the subject.

Might History, which Althusser always defined as a 'process without subject', be a 'tale told by an idiot, full of sound and fury'? His writings on psychoanalysis insist that the unconscious analyzes itself – which amounts to saying that no *outside* exists. That means there is no waste, either – no *remainder*. Analysis occurs as autophagy, an autarchic moment. As the social unconscious, or, rather, a repressive superego – a *fixative* destined to thwart individuation – ideology comprises an array of imaginary representations that reflect, in dazzling array, the tasks and positions of human beings in the social sphere. It has no *outside*, either. Instead, it addresses us *from behind*: the way the psychoanalyst speaks to the patient on the couch. 'You must never judge someone on the basis of his own self-conscious image but on the basis of the whole process which, behind this consciousness, produces it.'[24] Ideology, like the unconscious, occupies a position 'behind our backs'.

'Not to indulge in storytelling', Althusser writes, 'remains for me the one and only definition of

24   Louis Althusser, *Philosophy and the Spontaneous Philosophy of the Scientists* (London: Verso, 2012), 214.

materialism.'[25] Telling oneself tales means maintaining an illusion, or a bundle of illusions, that only serve to legitimate or explain our actions. This is what ideology does: it assures social cohesion by assigning individuals predetermined places, telling the 'story' (*histoire*) everyone is duty-bound to believe. But 'not to indulge in story-telling' means more than just changing the course of the narrative: it means breaking the mould where the truth is fabricated – cognizance of the fact that these 'stories' amount to circumstantial fictions, an ensemble of *a posteriori* justifications; that is, they cannot constitute an 'origin' in which a people or an individual might find support.

Dick pursued a similar objective in his novels when he expanded the contestation of 'reality' to time. Time, he explains, is not linear; it is 'orthogonal' and moves in different directions on a single axis, thereby producing multiple realities. It 'contains . . . as a simultaneous plane or extension, everything which was, just as grooves on an LP contain that part of the music which has already been played'.[26] We do not inhabit the universe just like that; rather, we live in a 'multiverse' prone to 'time-slips'. And they really do happen, Dick assures us. If we fail to notice such slips, it is because 'our brains automatically generate false memory-systems to obscure them'.[27] Time is energy invested in the infinite production of veils (*dokos*) assuring the coherence of reality and '[hiding] the ontological

25 Althusser, *The Future*, 221.
26 Philip K. Dick, *The Shifting Realities of Philip K. Dick: Selected Literary and Philosophical Writings*, ed. Lawrence Sutin (New York: Pantheon, 1995), 216.
27 Ibid., 216.

reality beneath its flow'.[28] Individuals, in turn, are nothing but 'stations' within 'a vast network'.[29]

As we know, the delirious discourse of the paranoiac approaches philosophical reflection – and to such an extent that the one can sometimes be mistaken for the other. 'Maybe', Dick observes, 'all systems – that is, any theoretical, verbal, symbolic, semantic, etc., formulation that attempts to act as an all-encompassing, all-explaining hypothesis of what the universe is about – are manifestations of paranoia.'[30] Inasmuch as any quest for insight may count as paranoid delirium, only the plausibility (*vraisemblance*) of its object allows us to distinguish between paranoia and philosophy, at least on an initial level. What do philosophers and paranoiacs say? In equal measure, they affirm that the disorder of life hides meaning. In either case, it is a matter of revealing order underlying the chaos of reality. The paranoiac is unmasked by the fact that he thinks the order is conspiratorial and directed against him. If the madman adopted Althusser's theory of history – the premise that it constitutes a 'process without subject' (that it is 'nothing personal', in other words) – wouldn't he turn into a full-blooded philosopher?

In discussing Alain Badiou, Slavoj Žižek speaks of a 'deceptive layer' that covers the real. This notion, which connects with the concept of alienation, underlies philosophical idealism: true life is elsewhere; *actual* reality is somewhere beyond appearances. As Joseph Heath and

28   Ibid., 217.
29   Ibid., 222.
30   Ibid., 208.

Andrew Potter demonstrate in *Nation of Rebels*,[31] the ideology of conspiracy fuelled 1960s counterculture. Such gnosticism attests to impotence, too: what can one do against a secret plot other than offer resistance in silence? Althusserian materialism rests on the certitude that reality has no *double*: everything is right there, before our eyes. The struggles are concrete, the forces at work stand in clear array, and the powers of illusion (i.e., ideology) are present inasmuch as institutions (*ideological state apparatuses*) materialize them. The decision 'not to indulge in storytelling' means the precise opposite of paranoia: reality is no longer divided into infinite paths leading towards a hidden truth. Clément Rosset, whom Althusser also taught, traces the matter to its source when he declares war on metaphysics – the search for a meaning beyond 'appearances'. The real is *idiotic*, he writes: 'that is, without doubling, existing in itself only'; '*idiotes* means simple, particular, unique'.[32] Metaphysical idealism such as one finds in conspiracy theories and films like *The Matrix* may be decoded as follows: 'its function is to protect the real; its structure is not a matter of refusing to perceive the real, but of doubling it; and its failure is to recognize only too late, in the protective double, the very real meant to be kept at bay [*dont on croyait s'être gardé*]'.[33] In other words, Althusser and Rosset position themselves at the opposite end of Philip K. Dick's

31   Joseph Heath and Andrew Potter, *Nation of Rebels: Why Counterculture Became Consumer Culture* (New York: HarperCollins, 2004).

32   Clément Rosset, *Traité de l'Idiotie* (Paris: Editions de Minuit, 1977), 42.

33   Clément Rosset, *Le Réel et son double* (Paris: Gallimard, 1993), 125.

'multiverse': ideology represents the very source of meta-physics; and their philosophical praxis involves lifting the scales from our eyes. The idiot and the madman join the philosopher in daring to declare that the emperor has no clothes . . .

The 'Mass Line' and Cultural Studies

Unsurprisingly, key figures in cultural studies such as Stuart Hall have stressed Althusser's 'impact' on the theories developed at the University of Birmingham during the 1960s and '70s. It is too readily forgotten that the theory of 'class struggle in philosophy', born of Althusser's exchanges with his Maoist students, paved the way for the study of popular culture. Among Althusserian concepts, Hall points to 'ideology as practices rather than as systems of ideas', and, moreover, to 'the ways in which Althusser . . . reshaped the central issue of the relationship between ideologies/culture and class formations'.[34] In effect – and in contradistinction to the tenets of classical Marxist thought – Althusser did not view relations between social groups and ideologies in terms of automatism. The one need not follow from the other, and 'class struggle in philosophy' pervades all discourses circulating in the social field. Most of all, Hall observes, Althusser advanced 'the argument that classes were not simple "economic" structures but formations constituted by *all*

---

34 Stuart Hall, 'Cultural Studies and the Centre: Some Problematics and Problems', in *Culture, Media, Language*, ed. Stuart Hall, Dorothy Hobson, Andrew Lowe and Paul Willis (London: Routledge, 1980), 21.

the different practices – economic, political, and ideological – and their effects on each other'.[35] In other words, and applied to the cultural sphere: the choice of a given sign of belonging does not make one the member of a given community; modalities of cultural production and consumption do not determine us; rather, the (system of) relations we establish between our practices and our choices assign us a 'position'. Here, *in nucleo*, lies the theoretical programme that presided over the genesis of *cultural studies*, the inaugural legitimation of the choice its practitioners made: to treat television programmes, comic books and popular singers with the same level of attention and seriousness as works of art belonging to the sphere of 'high culture' (or, as it was more commonly known at the time, 'bourgeois culture'). Among the founders of the Centre for Contemporary Cultural Studies at the University of Birmingham, Raymond Williams affirmed that 'cultural materialism' provided the basis for his critical project: 'comfort', entertainment and public opinion (or ideology) should receive as much attention as other phenomena – automobiles, say, or clothing.[36]

In the crucible of radical movements in the late 1960s, the Maoists of the UJC (Union des jeunesses communistes marxistes-léninistes) elaborated the theory of the 'mass line in philosophy'. Their leader, Robert Linhart, had been Althusser's pupil at the École Normale Supérieure. Mao Zedong codified the definition of the mass line as follows: *take the ideas of the masses and interpret them in light of Marxism-Leninism, then bring them back to the*

35 Ibid., 22.
36 See Raymond Williams, *Culture and Materialism: Selected Essays* (London: Verso, 2005).

masses. This cultural reading of the working class, the principle that the productions of the people prevail over all others, gave rise to a kind of inverted elitism. On the one hand, a given work was to be judged in terms of the interest the proletariat would show for it. On the other hand, every cultural expression of the working class should become the object of a painstaking decoding, in order to find the 'correct' interpretation of Marxist thought and better understand the people's message. As such, the 'mass line' represented a double hermeneutic: a theological *disputatio* in perpetuity, whereby 'the People' replaced 'God' in offering an ambiguous discourse with hidden intentions to be explored.

As such, what makes cultural studies and its artistic derivates the paradigm for contemporary thinking comes from remainders of Benjaminian messianism transfigured by Maoism and Althusserism. The metaphysical quest borne by revolutionary radicalism took refuge in the erudite deciphering of popular culture; by this means, the 'historical rescue' Benjamin once envisioned was supposed to occur. Since then, the 'masses' have transformed into consumer crowds, and Maoism has turned into postmodernist theory. For all that, the methods and the theoretical presuppositions prove astonishingly similar. 'Viewing knowledge in terms of the masses', as French Maoists urged, means affirming that the first criterion for judging a cultural production is its producer's status: membership in one social group or another legitimates, *in fine*, the content and the value of the production. Postcolonial theory, by way of cultural studies, directly inherited this 'mass line', which holds that the origin of a given production trumps all other considerations. Such is the grand, postmodern question: where are you from? To what social, ethnic, religious, sexual group do you belong? That said, for the French Maoists, the proletariat represented much more than an origin: it embodied the march of History, and there could be no doubt it would not remain minoritarian. 'At the starting-point of Maoist discourse', Jean-Claude Milner observes, 'one finds *massiveness*. It was a matter of starting with enormous entities: the People, the People's Cause, Proletarian Revolution, History. Then – and most often without any transition – came the details. Such-and-such an action, declaration, or circumstance.'[37]

In *Sogni d'Oro*, Nanni Moretti revisits his militant years. The film includes a sequence that explicitly refers to this 'mass line'. Various people tell the director that 'the Abruzzo shepherd, the Treviso housewife, and the Lucanian worker' will never understand a single word he says – consequently, his film holds no interest. However, one of the final scenes shows these figures of the people take the stage as actual characters; they board a train for Rome, burst into the projection booth, and declare that they love the movie. Individuals, Moretti affirms, are always in the right against those who assimilate them to a 'mass': ideology only seeks to transform a group, whatever it may be, into an instrumentalizable entity.

Contemporary artists, when they manipulate popular culture from a hermeneutic and critical perspective, ultimately inherit this 'mass line'. Cultural production offers an immense constellation of signs from heterogeneous spaces and times – or, to use another metaphorical register, a heap of rubble. Classifications and hierarchies

37 Jean-Claude Milner, *L'Arrogance du Présent. Regards sur une décennie, 1965–1975* (Paris: Grasset, 2009), 150.

belong to another universe: a world of norms, precalibrated formats and categories – in other words, all that stems from the fixative power of ideology. Since the 1970s, artistic and literary *canons* have counted as key battlefields for political correctness, feminism and postcolonialism. First dismembered and then reassembled, they reflect the advance of a 'mass line' whose principle has been inverted; now, *minorities* have replaced the working class as the motor of History, whose interests are at stake in political activism.

The mastery of the collective narrative stands at issue. In its name, Althusser barged into the meeting room at the PLM Saint-Jacques – to proclaim the forgotten kinship between the 'mass of analysands' and the proletariat. Also in its name, Foucault traced the genealogy of *madness*, starting with the 'great confinement' through which the mentally ill (individuals 'without history') wound up in asylums. Finally, in its name, Benjamin assigned the historian the task of 'rescue', whereby s/he endeavours to reconstitute, on the basis of the wreckage of the past, the morphology of ideas that majoritarian concepts have defeated, crushed and buried. These accounts – which run counter to *origins* affirmed by instances of power – all advance a vision of History starting from singular points, or accidents. That is, they twist the neck of the Ideal.

Everyone knows the Lacanian formula: 'the unconscious is structured like a language'. Because human societies are also unconscious productions (in part) – that is, because they emit, receive and transform signs – they are structured like a language, too. Cultural studies attests to the fact that each human society represents a way of *telling things* in the language of reality, articulating a position with respect to the world, and producing a *group subject* subordinate to four levels of the unthought: phantasmagoria, ideology, culture, the unconscious. The reality surrounding us is a fact of language, which artists must learn to master and articulate, along with all its symbols, metonymies, metaphors and repetitions. In particular, they must employ what 'falls out' in the process of enunciation, that is, its *waste*. Reading Joyce's *Ulysses*, Lacan devised a singular concept: the *sinthome*. This mental object comes into view as a detached piece; it separates from the rest of the brain and exists in a state of dysfunction, having no purpose other than to *impede individual functions*. In other words, it operates as a psychoanalytic *exform* . . .

Let us recall the feature shared by the philosopher and the paranoiac: for both, meaning lies hidden beneath the disorder of life. Truly paranoid thought is inseparable from this inaugural division, a *selective screening* it needs to meet its ends. In order to lay hold of his object, the paranoiac thinker excludes what encumbers him; he relegates sources of trouble to the realm of insignificance and casts into the shadows those elements that perturb his perspective and obstruct the arrival of the 'revelation' that promises to fulfil his desire. Such a dogged quest for meaning always entails a chiaroscuro dramaturgy, a world of contrast fuelled by exclusion. Accordingly, the paranoiac's passion for classification attests to an indifference to, if not hatred for, chaos – a panicked fear of the void. Needless to say, the world today seems to be teeming with people of this kind; they grow more and more active the more chaotic the universe that they inhabit becomes. In consequence, denying the chaos of culture begins when one identifies a corpus, a restricted canon that generates its counterpart automatically: a grey zone inhabited by 'insignificant' objects. Whatever principles attended its formation, the expulsion-machine is now up and running, hunting down *exforms*. From its beginnings under the sign of the nineteenth-century social and moral Ideal, it perpetuated itself over the course of the following age – first and foremost in an exacerbated fashion that culminated in *degenerate art*, before, in an attenuated manner, simply rejecting the 'insignificant', 'ugly' or 'subaltern'.

II
The Angel of the Masses

It is readily granted that art does not have the task of illustrating. But can art *make history*? If it weighs on human mentalities at all, art should count as an actor in History. Picasso did not think it enough to document the bombing of Guernica; rather, he translated a sense of indignation into form. The gesture that seeks to inscribe itself in History and the position the author assumes when confronting the latter should not be confused. Evaluating relations between money and politics means, first and foremost, defining the connection between event and form. Contrary to what the majority of 'radical' theorists today claims, form is not subordinate to discourse either; for instance, the pictorial system Jacques-Louis David set up influenced the politics of his times just as much as politics influenced his art. In 1913, Marcel Duchamp exhibited his first readymade; in 1917, Kazimir Malevich painted *White on White*. To be sure, these works were products of historical circumstances; equally, however, they were *events* that irreversibly modified what followed. Although they started out as consequences, they became first causes and brought forth manifold effects in other artists and works; in turn, these effects spread and came to be part of the atmosphere of a general sensibility. Accordingly, we will confront two entirely divergent versions of art history in the following. The first insists on discourse and claims that artistic forms represent the product of the social and political context in which they emerge. The second emphasizes form, affirming that each great work forms a 'crucible of the event' (Alain Badiou); when one examines it in context, a particular chain of collisions becomes evident. In this perspective, the fundamental relation between art and History proves a matter of ongoing interaction extending in two directions at once: Duchampian readymades and Malevich's painting, like all works of art, modify past and future alike.

The present is uncertain by nature – forever *flashing* and oscillating between the traces left by History and the potential they contain. Art lends such incertitude a positive charge: underscoring the precarity of the historical moment, it induces a state of active lucidity in the observer, which proves inseparable from political action. The permanent rereading of hierarchies and values conducted in the framework of cultural studies – which seeks to extract social significance from mass production or popular artistic expressions – participates in the permanent struggle against reification. Such perpetual movement – which acts on our vision of History, artistic practices and relation to the *polis* – incarnates a new messenger to be called, following Benjamin's 'Angel of History', the *Angel of the Masses*. Arising from the abstract systems that surround us and descending from the leaden clouds of ideology overhead, this messenger brings news of a *non-massive* world: a historical record comprising accidents, grains of sand and singularities. In a universe of crowded statistics, computerized clouds and treks through chaos, the *Angel of the Masses* circulates between works of art in the form of circuits and networks; incarnating transcoding and translation, it roams everywhere that a renewed relationship between art and politics is manifest under the aegis of the aleatory and the *accidental*.

History and Accident

By portraying the actors of the French Revolution as if they were mythological heroes, Jacques-Louis David fastened the nascent Republic to the moral values and visual imaginary of ancient Rome. He thereby contributed to revolutionary ideology in decisive fashion by translating the very *form* of its politics, making it declamatory, oratorical, marmoreal, and fixed like ancient statuary. In most of David's paintings, the event contains its own monument: it stands before History, and sometimes even proves to have already been historicized, i.e., legendary. Michel Thévoz has observed that the revolutionary bourgeoisie, in contrast to the aristocracy or proletariat,

> has no legitimacy before or after itself; it is irrevocably the transitory class . . . If it wishes to perpetuate itself, then, it must recur to contraceptive measures. It can only save itself by frigidity or sterility. Hence this fascination for marble, lifeless stone, funereal matter that freezes time and sculpts immortality. First of all,

> Woman, the embodiment of desire and the threat of life, must be transformed into a statue.[1]

Such is the paradigm of the *bourgeois* in art: to give life's disorder the thick consistency of the mineral, to paint what stands with a varnish of eternity on which its power – the power of *idealization*, above all – will then rest. This quality still holds in our own day; one can easily distinguish, in contemporary artistic practice, between works that present the world as it is and works that depict it in its ideal form – that is, covered with an ideology aiming to make the present state of things *tolerable*.

According to psychoanalysis, the way we fashion an account of our life depends, at a primary level, on so-called *identity*, that is, on the image we forge of ourselves – our *ego ideal*. Psychoanalysis permits one to reorganize this narrative on the basis of associations between unforeseen ideas. The past is reread not in light of a preconceived image – which commonly starts with our 'origins' – but in terms of the 'real' of experience, in the Lacanian sense: what offers resistance and cannot be grasped directly; it involves visiting the shadowy realms the unconscious harbours and learning its peculiar linguistics, its grammatical logic. Significantly, the same holds for collective narratives – above all, for any vision of History. History may vary enormously from one country to the next inasmuch as it is oriented on the political interests of the moment and the founding myths of a given community. Like the scenario of our individual lives, History offers both a map, a representation drawn in keeping with

---

1   Michel Thévoz, *Le Théâtre du crime. Essai sur la peinture de David* (Paris: Minuit, 1989), 40.

information gathered, and a montage – here, one must ask who has been authorized to make the 'final cut'. Orson Welles may well have filmed all the shots in *The Magnificent Ambersons*, but RKO Studios, which held the legal rights, distorted their arrangement to such an extent that the director finally repudiated the work. Who signs for the final montage of our existence – and for the narrative of History?

'Historical idealism' names the idea that an exterior instance, of whatever kind, has the right to make this *final cut* – and even if it occurs to the detriment of the individuals or groups over which its authority extends. When this happens, History is endowed with a precise meaning. Such a teleology may be more or less disguised, but it aims to legitimate a political strategy. In the Eastern Bloc, a veritable screenplay accompanied historical montage: the working class, playing the protagonist, would ultimately triumph when a truly egalitarian society arrived – perfected communism, which always lay somewhere in the distant future. The screenplay applied to modern art, too. Here, the same teleology extended to the domain of forms – e.g., Clement Greenberg's narrative, which describes how painting progresses towards a fuller and fuller realization of its intrinsic properties. Other critics have oriented the narrative on the 'end of art': when life, liberated from the division of labour, absorbs it entirely. Modernism – and the twentieth century in general – is characterized by the (paranoid) idea that the present belongs to a global screenplay assuring its 'meaning'. Such belief in the 'anteriority of meaning' vis-à-vis the real as it is lived (to employ Althusser's expression) amounts, alternatively, to an authoritarian phantasm or to a quest in vain. Either way, it involves searching for *origins* and *ends* to justify the present. 'As Walter Benjamin judiciously observes', Siegfried Kracauer wrote, 'the idea of a progress of humanity is untenable mainly for the reason that it is insolubly bound up with the idea of chronological time as the matrix of a meaningful process'.[2] If History is determined by some kind of necessity – if it amounts to a global screenplay in which every actor must play a part – then art can enter the picture only in a reflective capacity, as an illustration.

Art's historical function – and therefore its political function, too – has substance only on a stage open to purely contingent human history; at very least, it requires the productive aporia of chance and necessity meeting in opposition. In his essay on 'the materialism of the encounter', Althusser enlists the Epicurean theory of falling atoms (*clinamen*) for his vision of History. The void represents the very condition for political action; accordingly, he rereads Marx's works in order to 'invent' the philosophy the latter 'did not have the time to write'. A gap opens up between the 'young Marx', whose thought was still shaped by Hegelian dialectics, and the Marx of later years, whose *Capital* inaugurated a 'science of History'. Althusser seeks to fill it by situating Marxist thought in what he calls the 'underground current of the materialism of the encounter', or *aleatory materialism*. In the process, he sets himself in opposition to *dialectical materialism*, which, he claims, merely amounts to idealism in disguise. Althusser's term follows the 'line of Democritus': History as a series of collisions and accidents, some of

2   Siegfried Kracauer, *History: The Last Things Before the Last* (Princeton: Markus Wiener Publishers, 1969), 149–50.

which constitute embryonic links of causality, while others have no lasting consequence.

One of the most representative authors of this *aleatory* current is Machiavelli, who conceived politics in terms of encounters that may occur – or may not:

> It is in the political *void* that the encounter must come about, and that national unity must 'take hold'. But *this political void is first a philosophical void.* No Cause that precedes its effects is to be found in it . . . One reasons here not in terms of the Necessity of the accomplished fact, but in terms of the contingency of the fact to be accomplished.[3]

History occurs as a succession of conjunctions and disjunctions without origin or end. For Machiavelli, political action occupies a *desert*, the perpetual site of 'beginnings'. Thus, in the film of the same name, the 'Matrix', in which the simulacra governing human life are generated hails the protagonist Neo with the words: 'Welcome to the desert of the real'. This is what defines the void in our age: society is a simulacrum, decisions are made in a vague *elsewhere*, all political action seems in vain . . . The subject at the centre of contemporary history is politically irresponsible, stripped of the potential to influence the world and caught up in a sense of emptiness which – *contra* Althusser's claim – cannot be identified as the site of 'beginnings'. To be able to act, then, one must view the real as a *void*. All political action starts here, in a dead zone.

3 Louis Althusser, *Philosophy of the Encounter: Later Writings, 1978–1987*, trans. G. M. Goshgarian (London: Verso, 2006), 174.

But if all action occurs in vain, if the Empire defies contestation, and if nothing can alter the order of things, it becomes all the more urgent to seek to transform it here and now. Just as Machiavelli's *Prince* declared that Italy could be unified starting from nothing, Althusser claims that a revolutionary party can win power by setting out with just an arsenal of ideas. Philosophy represents a '*Kampfplatz*', a battleground where thinking transforms into wartime strategy: 'it has no absolute beginning; in consequence, it can – indeed, should – begin with anything at all'. Suddenly, then, philosophy lacks an *object*, properly speaking. It is nothing but the modulation of the eternal conflict between two tendencies: materialism and idealism. And if 'philosophical objects' exist after all, they entertain no relation with real objects; instead, they resonate with two fields that provide philosophical thinking its sole index in reality: science and politics. One might also add art and love – as Alain Badiou would later do.

To oppose a system, one must first conceive its nature as *precarious*. Doing so implies waking from a kind of hypnosis, breaking through the marmoreal representations imposed by the conservative bourgeoisie, and seeing the operative system as a fragile *installation* – a spectacle that ideology has transformed into a reality. The components of capitalism, Althusser explains, exist '*in a "floating" state* prior to their "accumulation" and "combination", each being the product of its own history, and none being the teleological product of the others or their history'.[4] Consequently, adherents of the 'line of Democritus' see only what results from the encounter

4   Ibid., 198.

between 'the owner of money', who has capital at his disposal, and the 'proletarian stripped of everything', who accepts lending the force of his labour in exchange for remuneration. What ensues is simply a chain reaction.

Fittingly, innumerable science fiction films portray the present as a laboratory experiment gone wrong; the story of capitalism, like that of the Soviet Union, could be told in the manner of *Twelve Monkeys*. Here, we see a *political* struggle between representations: on the one hand, the state of things appears as a swarm of tiny accidents in perpetual instability, subject to the regime of the aleatory; on the other hand, the standing order seems to be eternal or simply 'the way things are', and nothing, evidently, can shake it. From the standpoint of power, the historical narrative will always be marmoreal; it has been sculpted with a will to idealize past and present alike. Nothing can unsettle this power more than the display of ruins, scattered debris, and images of fragility which contemporary artists extract from the archives: their provocation takes aim at the *defensive illusionism* proclaiming the order of things stems from ineluctable fatality.

This 'philosophy for Marxism' that Althusser sought to produce – *aleatory materialism* amounting to a war machine against 'disguised forms of idealism' – brings to the fore a school of thought that has been neglected, to say the least. *Nominalism* is not merely 'the antechamber of materialism', as Marx contended; it is 'materialism itself'. Althusser finds an emblematic formulation in Wittgenstein's *Tractatus Logico-Philosophicus*: 'Die Welt ist alles, was der Fall ist' – in other words, and as he translated it, 'the world is everything that happens', or, more literally, 'the world is everything that befalls us'. Yet another rendition exists, from the school of Bertrand Russell: 'The world is everything that is *the case*.'[5] Brought to bear on twentieth-century aesthetic debates, the world of art constitutes the field of nominalism *par excellence*, if not its purest expression: it consists entirely of particular *cases*, constantly redrawing borders by wearing away at defining categories and the norms on which they rest. Does any other sphere of knowledge correspond so fully to the description of nominalism – that is, a world 'consist[ing] exclusively of singular, unique objects, each with its own specific name and singular properties'?[6] Moreover, Althusser observes, language (*le verbe*) already constitutes an abstraction: 'We would have to be able to speak without words, that is, to show. This indicates the primacy of the gesture over the word, of the material trace over the sign.'[7] As such, artistic practice represents spontaneous nominalism; its expressive register, which accords greater and greater significance to gestures and 'material traces', matches Althusser's and Benjamin's visions of History completely.

From the perspective of Althusserian materialism, the world as it stands arises from innumerable collisions occasioned by the 'infinitesimal deviation' of atoms on parallel trajectories: in essence, it is *accidental*. It forms a *climate* (*conjoncture*) – that is, a unique disposition of elements and events in space and time. In his 'Theses on the Philosophy of History', Benjamin, drawing inspiration from Paul Klee's painting, *Angelus Novus*, sketches the portrait of what this figure embodies: *the Angel of*

---

5   Ibid., 265.
6   Ibid.
7   Ibid.

History. 'His face is turned toward the past', he writes. 'Where we perceive a chain of events, he sees one single catastrophe which keeps piling wreckage upon wreckage and hurls it in front of his feet.'[8] A cloud bursts and carries off the angel: 'This storm', Benjamin concludes, 'is what we call progress.' All by itself, the image sums up the materialist conception of History: a succession of collisions and chance assemblages, wreckage left by the struggles of yesterday, fragments whose *legibility* must now be assured. Stuart Hall also views Marxism from this catastrophic perspective: it strikes him as absurd to think, as Marx did, that 'capitalism evolved organically from within its own transformations'; he explains: 'I came from a society where the profound integument of capitalist society, economy, and culture had been imposed by conquest and colonization.'[9] Today, European history can be written starting with the ruins left by colonial wars; the economic stakes of Golden Age Dutch painting, for instance, are most readily discerned from the standpoint of the contemporary culture industry. Tomorrow, who knows what point of view will offer the best way to revisit the ruins of the world today?

Paradoxically, Slavoj Žižek endorses Althusser's position by way of commentary on Hegel – whose historical idealism stands at the antipodes of this aleatory vision of the world *a priori*. Historical necessity, he affirms, is posterior to chance: 'necessity is always retroactive. Of course there is a necessity at work, but this necessity

---

8 Walter Benjamin, *Illuminations*, trans. Harry Zohn (New York: Harcourt Brace Jovanovich, 2007), 257.

9 Stuart Hall, *Critical Dialogues in Cultural Studies* (London: Routledge, 1996), 264.

always arises at the end, as contingent.'[10] In other words, History is aleatory; we discover meaning in it as it unfolds, or after the fact. Althusser correctly maintains that '*every process is governed by its end*'.[11] As such, it is pointless to try to determine where the 'objective tendency' of History stands in order to contribute to its realization – as Marx sought to do. On the contrary, 'through our actions we construct the necessity that will determine us retroactively'.[12] Through this lens, every work of art affects both the past and the future: a site of temporal bifurcation, it opens paths that other artists will walk down and, at the same time, offers a perspective for rereading the past. Jorge Luis Borges expresses the same idea when he evokes 'Kafka's precursors': every great *oeuvre* invents its own genealogy and creates a new history of literature in reverse. In other words – and to use the term devised by OULIPO (*Ouvroir de Littérature potentielle*) – artistic and literary history consists of innu-merable 'plagiarists by anticipation'. The work of art operates on both directions of time: turning towards the future, it generates its own causal chain; plunging into the past, it modifies the form and content of History. Every work, then, constitutes a *bifurcation*: as in Borges's short stories, its present is *undecidable*, tracing lines of flight from one pole of chronology to the other.

The history of art, then, may be read either from left to right or from right to left. Far from exhibiting idealism or mysticism of any sort, its *timeless* character reaches in both

10   Slavoj Žižek, *A travers le réel* (Paris: Éditions Lignes, 2010), 48.
11   Louis, Althusser, *Writings on Psychoanalysis: Freud and Lacan*, trans. Jeffrey Melman (New York: Columbia University, Press, 1999), 57.
12   Žižek, *A travers le réel*, 49.

directions extending from the present. The *undecidable character* of the work of art renders all teleology null and void: assigning any historical finality at all to art means denying the idea of movement and replacing it with a scenario scripted in advance. Assigning an *origin* involves a similar negation, for art's historical foundations are in perpetual movement, too; archaeology yields only infinite excavation – just as risky, uncertain and complex as the paths of the future. 'As flowers turn toward the sun,' Benjamin wrote, 'what has been strives to turn – by dint of a secret heliotropism – toward that sun which is rising in the sky of history.'[13] This is why Stuart Hall can read the history of capitalism in light of a new 'sun': postcolonialist thought.

Althusser notes a striking formula in the first version of Marx's *Critique of Political Economy*: 'The anatomy of the ape does not explain that of man, rather human anatomy contains a key to the anatomy of the ape.' The statement commands his attention for two reasons:

> first, because it precludes in advance any teleological interpretation of an evolutionist conception of history. In the second place, it literally anticipates, though clearly in different circumstances, Freud's theory of deferred action, whereby the significance of an earlier affect is recognised only in and via a subsequent one.[14]

Via this notion of *belatedness*, the writing of History and psychoanalysis meet up in the realm of art. Not only is the past incessantly reactivated by the present – moreover,

---

13 Benjamin, *Illuminations*, 255.
14 Louis Althusser, *The Future Lasts Forever: A Memoir*, trans. Richard Veasey (New York: The New Press, 1995), 208.

the very nature of 'necessity' (which is supposed to steer it) is subject to the vagaries of the present. The work of art does not offer formal content alone; it also presents a corresponding interpretive and historical context: that is, it produces genealogies as well as outlooks. For any artist at all, then, situating oneself in a political space signifies, first and foremost, choosing the historical narrative within which she or he positions and deploys his or her work.

It is generally agreed that no particular style dominates our age. This impression may follow from the voluminous quantity of contemporary artistic productions – which only enhances its heteroclite allure. Perhaps the incipient twenty-first century will be recognized *a posteriori* as having been traversed by stylistic figures, motifs and representations that, while spontaneous, are sufficiently defined to present a vision of space and time just as consistent as *quattrocento* geometries or the ethereal volutes of eighteenth-century France. If one duly observes artistic production today, it is clear that human societies do not appear as organic totalities so much as disparate ensembles of structures, institutions and social practices detachable from each other – and which, most commonly, qualify as specific to different 'cultures'. The corollary of this atomized vision of the social sphere is the evolution of yesterday's unitary political struggle (revolutionary Marxism) towards multiple combats in discrete sectors and communities. Indeed, the nation-state no longer counts as a totality to be reworked from top to bottom – the potential object of a revolutionary *tabula rasa*. Like atmospheric pollution, the flow of capital refuses to acknowledge political borders.

As much is plain not just in works of art, but in Hollywood cinema. What is customarily called 'reality' has no more consistency than a *montage*. Starting from this observation, one may view artistic practice as a kind of software permitting action to be performed on communal reality in order to produce alternative versions of the same. That is, contemporary art *post-produces* social reality: by formal means, it illuminates the montages constituting it – which are formal, too. Thus, one of the essential elements of contemporary art's political programme is that of *bringing the world into a precarious state* – in other words, constantly affirming the *transitory* and *circumstantial* nature of the institutions that structure social life, the rules governing individual and collective behaviour. After all, the ideological apparatuses of capitalism proclaim the very opposite. They declare the political and economic framework in which we are living to be immutable and definitive: a scenario in which the décor and props undergo perpetual (and superficial) transformation – but nothing else changes. The central political task of contemporary art does not involve denouncing any current 'political' fact in particular. Instead, the point is to bring precarity to mind: to keep the notion alive that *intervention* in the world is possible, to propagate the creative potential of human existence in all its forms. It is because social reality constitutes an *artifact* through and through that we can imagine changing it. Art exposes the world's non-definitive character. It dislocates, disassembles and hands things over to disorder and poetry. By producing representations and counter-models that underscore the intrinsic fragility of the standing order, art bears the standard of a political project that is much more efficient (in the sense of generating concrete effects) and much more ambitious (inasmuch as it concerns all aspects of political reality) than it would be if it simply relayed a watchword or ideology.

Thus, inasmuch as our world is nothing but a pure construction – an ideological arrangement (or 'phantasmagoria', in Benjamin's terms) – it stands as the theatre for a struggle between different narratives and fictions. Jacques Rancière seems to draw an analogous conclusion when he writes that 'the relationship between art and politics [is] not a passage from fiction to reality, but a relationship between two ways of making a fiction'.[15] Althusser made this question the very cornerstone of ideology. When he defines ideology as a 'representation of the real' that is 'distorted, . . . biased, and tendentious' inasmuch as it aims to 'keep individuals in the place determined by class domination',[16] he foregrounds that a given social fiction exists only through its actors' participation, the regulated movement of extras; ideology is a screenplay that 'interpellates' characters without end. For Althusser, the repressive fiction undergirding the social scenario is relayed by an immense network of instruments he calls 'ideological state apparatuses' (ISA) – to distinguish them from state power as such, which is inherently and immediately identifiable. ISAs have no need for armed force because they 'function by ideology':[17] they are religious, scholastic, familial, cultural, juridical and

---

15   Jacques Rancière, *Le Spectateur émancipé* (Paris: La Fabrique, 2008), 84. [Trans: Not included in English-language edition; a different version of the essay, without the quoted passage, is found in *Dissensus: On Politics and Aesthetics* (London: Bloomsbury, 2010).]

16   Quoted in Jacques Rancière, *Althusser's Lesson*, trans. Emiliano Battista (London: Bloomsbury, 2011), 135.

17   Louis Althusser, *Lenin and Philosophy and Other Essays*, trans. Ben Brewster (London: Verso, 1971), 97.

informational . . . In a word – given that the state, in 'bourgeois' societies, 'is the precondition for any distinction between public and private'[18] – they are all instances of power. These apparatuses have the objective of 'reproducing relations of production' as they stand. Hence the pre-eminence Althusser grants the educational apparatus, the heart of ideological fabrication.[19] What he meant to demonstrate – the idea that now provides the theoretical foundation for cultural studies – is that ideology possesses 'material existence'.[20] In other words, ideas occurring to an individual are actualized by behaviours; ideology is reflected in practice: the 'material rituals' that structure our social and cultural life by lending concrete form to the collective screenplay. A given society is shaped through a narrative that yields scripts and *casts roles* in a vast array of scenes.

Heterochronies

How does this aleatory vision of History translate into the sphere of artistic composition? Rosalind Krauss has observed that Renaissance perspective was 'the visual correlate of causality' inasmuch as 'one thing follows the next in space according to rule'. But if modernist painting did away with a centred, monocular perspective and affirmed the flatness of pictorial space, it also, and above all, replaced it with 'a temporal perspective, i.e., history'.[21]

18   Ibid., 97.
19   Ibid., 104.
20   Ibid., 113–14.
21   Rosalind Krauss, 'A View of Modernism', *Artforum*, September 1972.

Essentially historical – ordered by the idea of social and artistic *progress* – modernist painting simply transposed, into time, the mental, logical and rational order through which Renaissance humanism had assured its mastery of the physical world; it is based on a historical narrative that situates works at determinate locations, 'the ones behind the others'. Here, the notion of history is synonymous with perspective; it amounts to its translation onto a temporal plane. In the age of the internet, communication occurring in real time, and global hypermobility, it seems only logical that new modes of perceiving and represent-ing space and time have emerged, prompting artists to weave the one into the other: as visual Moebius strips – semiotic chains combining the features of different media and formats – made possible by computer technology. Immersed in a universe of permanent 'visual shocks', whose premises Benjamin articulated long ago, the sensi-bility of the twenty-first-century individual is evolving towards an imaginary of multiplicity and reticulation.[22] To be sure, it would be excessive to pretend that a specific form dominates contemporary art, given its formal and conceptual profusion. All the same, the presence of the network-structure and its derivatives pervades artistic production too much to amount to a mere 'tendency'. The horizon of the present, both conceptually and visually, seems to be dominated by pulverization, scattering and links. Clusters, clouds, tree structures, constellations, webs, archipelagos . . . All these forms evoke pixels – as if to signal the decomposable structure of the universe and the precarious nature of our political systems.

22   On this question, see Nicolas Bourriaud, *The Radicant* (Berlin: Sternberg Press, 2009) and *Altermodern* (London: Tate Britain, 2009).

The primary concern for contemporary aesthetics, its central problematic, is organizing multiplicity: relations outweigh objects, branches points, and passages presence; paths prove more significant than the stations along the way. And so, inasmuch as they are caught up in dynamic contexts, forms naturally tend to exude (*secréter*) narratives: concerning first their production, then their diffusion. As such, works present themselves as complex structures capable of generating forms before, during and after their realization. The predominance of multiplicity has the corollary of a *heterochronic* conception of time: beyond the 'pure presence' and momentariness that distinguish the modernist work as a world-unto-itself, contemporary art postulates multiple temporalities – a representation of time evoking the *constellation*. In like fashion, a supernova we see in the sky turns out to have been dead for millions of years – the light that is visible proves to be just a remainder; we are contemplating time more than space. The constellation's specificity is its heterochronic character: it comprises an ensemble of stars, whose rays seem close enough to be connected by imaginary lines yielding figures. But if the stars constituting the constellation seem to be close, in fact they lie light years apart in three-dimensional space. A constellation – an 'asterism' – is a figure constructed through formal analogy, an arbitrary object given shape by connecting scattered elements, a *folding* of space and time. In the process, motifs emerge, which then receive titles such as 'Orion', 'Leo', or 'Ursa Major'; for all that, they are *coups de force* the imagination performs on reality. Such work is *semionautic* – a term I have used to describe dynamic articulation: an artistic gesture, to realize a form, linking a multiplicity of scattered signs or the actions constituting a pattern of behaviour.[23]

The ubiquity of reticular forms in contemporary art – and, more particularly, the constellation-motif and its derivates – stems from technological advances, especially modes of reading and mental displacement brought about by the internet. However, the causes are also sociological – indeed, civilizational.[24] From Andreas Gursky's Photoshopped pictures, saturated with detail, to pullulating installations by Sarah Sze, Jason Rhoades, Jim Shaw and Mike Kelley that draw on proliferating archives and displays of objects and images – not to mention the clouds of information and data that painters such as Franz Ackermann and Julie Mehretu use when composing their works – the *heterogeneous* has come to govern the current regime of visibility. The same is even more apparent in music, where the dominant mode of composition involves grafting together elements that belong to different epochs or cultures. Above all, this enduring trend is due to the saturation of consumer space: hyper-production, combined with hyper-archiving, sets the individual adrift in a warehouse which assumes the form of a labyrinth.

Panicked by the profusion of cultural offerings and the colossal dimensions of all that is to be surveyed, we focus less on the space we happen to occupy than on any thread

23   Nicolas Bourriaud, *Formes de vie* (Paris: Denoël, 1999).

24   In American television series especially attuned to the spirit of the times during the 2000s, the motor of the plot often proved to be a temporal operator, a conceptual switchboard – e.g., the basement of the abandoned hovel in *Lost*, where a rudder moves the island in space and time, or the pinboard in *FlashForward*, which the investigator uses to link clues and reconstruct thirty seconds of collective blackout, when humanity was projected into the future. In *Homeland*, the CIA agent also sets up a pinboard in her apartment.

of Ariadne that seems to promise a way out. Hence the importance, in contemporary culture, of links, charts, guides and navigational narratives. Likewise, this accounts for the prominence of agents of orientation and checking (*récolement*): DJs, programmers, curators, compilers, iconographers, 'buyers' and editors – a veritable universe of professionals who establish relations between things and engineer experience.[25] In a sociocultural context marked by super-production and infinite archiving, the *trajectory* – as a lived experience offered to a public – has come to constitute an artistic form in its own right. I have attempted to describe this family of *trajectory-forms* – albeit from the overly reductive perspective of voyage and displacement – in my essay *Radicant*. Here, I refer to the general *viatorization* of cultural signals that emerged as a counterpoint to economic globalization in the 2000s and planted the seed for forms exiled beyond the limits of the ascendant cultural Empire; indeed, it has come to provide the mental threshold for a nascent planetary modernity one might call 'altermodern'.

That said, the constellation-form calls for reflection on a larger scale. A singular item bathed in a remarkable aura attests as much: art historian Aby Warburg's *Atlas Mnemosyne*. Intended as a cognitive tool for identifying the deep logic that holds between heterogeneous images, this atlas comprised over two thousand reproductions on seventy-nine boards when its creator died in 1929. Each of the 'screens' – constellations c

---

25 On this subject, see Nicolas Bourriaud, *Postproduction* (P␣ Sternberg Press, 2002). For the musical domain, see Simon Re␣ *Retromania* (New York: Faber & Faber, 2011).

black-and-white images against a black background –
offers a host of thematic and formal connections, often
obscure. Warburg inaugurated a veritable epistemological rupture by pursuing historical analysis based on
iconography. Placing the image at the centre of the cognitive process enabled him to deploy a mode of thinking
that worked through staging (*didascalies*), channels
(*chaînages*) and combination (*combinatoires*). The
method governing this enterprise, as well as the aesthetic
it entails, have made the *Atlas Mnemosyne* a kind of
monument that is fully *legible* only in our own times. By
decades, Warburg anticipated interdisciplinary iconographic research, pursuit of analogies, and *browsing* that
contemporary artists prize – in other words, the common
denominator of cultural experience today.

Giorgio Agamben has noted the *energetic* conception
of images in Warburg's project. Here, he writes, 'is the
crystallization of an energetic charge and an emotional
experience that survive as an inheritance transmitted by
social memory and that, like electricity condensed in a
Leyden jar, become effective only through contact with
the "selective will" of a particular period'.[26] Each symbol
constitutes a 'dynamogram', delivering a charge that
varies in accordance with the context in which it is situ-
ated: works evolve with time and space. Warburg juxta-
posed reproductions of art and advertising brochures,
details of sculptures and snapshots of Hopi Indians or
people walking down the street in American towns. In the
same space, Delacroix's *Medea* meets up with a woman

---

26 Giorgio Agamben, *Potentialities: Collected Essays in
Philosophy*, trans. Daniel Heller-Roazen (Stanford: Stanford University
1999), 94.

playing golf, drawings by Renaissance astrologists, and medieval illuminations . . . If the system of thinking that Warburg set up represents the object of such fascination today, this is because it corresponds to the dominant visual matrix of our epoch. Networks, maps, charts, diagrams and constellations feature in contemporary art because they share a *reticular* structure: an array of points connected with each other by links, whether the latter are visible or not. Their raw material is, in essence, visual *information*, akin to the logic of 'browsing' that internet users employ when clicking from one site to another. Such information – or, more accurately, coding – does not translate into the same thing in every context. The contemporary fortunes of the *Atlas Mnemosyne* stem from its insistence on the dynamic nature of forms – the specific energy locating them in a heterochronic temporality that changes from one epoch to the next in keeping with the way they are *downloaded* into different contexts. Art is a 'dynamogram': an inscription programmed for time travel. Marcel Duchamp described his *Bride Stripped Bare by Her Bachelors, Even* as a 'delay in glass'. Every work is ontologically *late*, and we perceive it only in bursts diffracted by the context through which we become aware of it.

Because it lacks continuity, our epoch is characterized by intermittent temporalities: a great kaleidoscope where pasts, presents and futures scintillate in furtive 'flashes'. Art historian George Kubler, fascinated as much by Robert Smithson's 'ruins in reverse' as by Aztec culture, confirms this analysis. 'Actuality', he writes,

is when the lighthouse is dark between flashes: it is the instant between the ticks of the watch: it is a void interval slipping forever through time . . . Yet the instant of actuality is all we ever can know directly. The rest of time emerges only in signals relayed to us at this instant by innumerable stages and by unexpected bearers. These signals are like kinetic energy stored until the moment of notice . . .[27]

Benjamin associated the *constellation* with a general concept of history's 'legibility' (*Lesbarkeit*): it relates to *divination*, the ancient science of prophetic interpretation. Starting with a particular detail (or set of details), the interpreter connects different temporalities in order to arrive at a view that amounts to prediction in reverse, prophecy turned towards the past. Such a mode of reading has been termed *asterochronic* – it 'establishes connections between events that are heterogeneous in time and space'.[28]

'Clues', Carlo Ginzburg's seminal essay from 1979, describes the emergence of the 'evidential paradigm' at the end of the nineteenth century: a model of knowledge based on signs that seem utterly unimportant. 'Infinitesimal traces', Ginzburg writes, 'permit the comprehension of a deeper, otherwise unattainable reality'.[29] This model emerged in the field of art history and in turn inspired psychoanalysis, yet it may also be discerned in detective fiction and philosophy. Like Giovanni Morelli's essays on

27   George Kubler, *The Shape of Time: Remarks on the History of Things* (New Haven: Yale University Press, 2008), 15.

28   Muriel Pic, 'La Fiction par les traces', *WGS* (Paris: L'inculte, 2011), 156.

29   Carlo Ginzburg, *Clues, Myths, and the Historical Method*, trans. John Tedeschi and Anne C. Tedeschi (Baltimore: Johns Hopkins University Press, 2013), 92.

Italian painting, the novels of Arthur Conan Doyle feature a mode of thinking that focuses on matters normally consigned to the margins – or neglected outright. Thus, in the realm of art, the least important parts of a work – details the painter executes mechanically and, as it were, unthinkingly (hair, nails, the shape of an ear or a finger . . .) – allowed Morelli to assign it to a particular artist.

Comprising symptoms, clues and pictorial signs, the 'evidential paradigm' derives from medical interpretation and diagnostic science as much as from the detective's patient craft. Ginzburg traces it back to the ancient practice of hunting – deciphering the mute and seemingly imperceptible tracks of animals – as well as the concept of *symptom* in Hippocratic medicine. By the same token, *evidential knowledge* shares traits with the most ancient divinatory methods – and to such an extent that Ginzburg speaks of 'retrospective prophecies' in Sherlock Holmes's dazzling intuitions and Morelli's claims. But while divination 'analyze[s] footprints, stars, feces, sputum, corneas, pulsations, snow-covered fields, or cigarette ashes'[30] in order to predict the future, the evidential method examines the same in order to reconstruct the past. This is also why Aby Warburg considered the historian of art a 'necromancer' capable of reviving traits of the past in the forms of the present. 'Morelli', Ginzburg writes, 'set out to identify, within a culturally conditioned system of signs such as the pictorial, those which appeared to be involuntary, as is the case with symptoms':[31] in other words, one finds an artist's signature in traces that

30   Ibid., 107.
31   Ibid.

display no intention at all (minor elements, scribblings, or the way hair or hands are painted).

Needless to say, such focus on *unconscious detail* leads us back to psychoanalysis. In 'The Moses of Michelangelo', Freud acknowledged his debt to Morelli; starting in the early 1880s, he read his articles on the Italian Renaissance, which appeared under the pseudonym 'Ivan Lermolieff'. Morelli's method is 'closely related to the technique of psycho-analysis', which 'is accustomed to divine secret and concealed things from unconsidered or unnoticed details, from the rubbish heap, as it were, of our observations'.[32] This 'rubbish heap' of observation, both historical and medical, provides the raw material of psychoanalysis. In the 1930s, the same register of the devalued and the rejected – albeit in terms of society and culture – offered unforetold objects of study to Siegfried Kracauer and Walter Benjamin: detective novels, hotel foyers and cabaret spectacles to the one; Parisian arcades, cinema and children's books to the other.

Rubble

In the second half of the 1950s, *Nouveau Réalisme* undertook the vast project of performing an archaeology of the present by way of the vagaries of mass production and the social use that objects found. Jacques de la Villeglé's work – an 'urban comedy' about French history since the end of the Second World War as related by the

32 Sigmund Freud, 'The Moses of Michelangelo', *Collected Papers* (New York: Basic, 1959), 4: 270–1; quoted in Ginzburg, *Clues*, 99.

'anonymous wounded' of advertising bills – emblematizes the aesthetics of *recuperation*. Benjamin Buchloh considered that Villeglé's works, as well as those of Raymond Hains and Mimmo Rotella, offered a radical interrogation of the artist in light of the social 'group-subject'. Villeglé, he argued, had introduced an entirely new attitude towards art: 'By consciously denying the traditional role, [the artist] yields to a collective gesture of productivity that, in historical context, amounts to mute aggression toward the state of alienation that has been imposed.'[33] This notion of 'anonymous production', Buchloh continues, paved the way for the approaches of Stanley Brouwn, Marcel Broodthaers and Bernd and Hilla Becher. Once the notion of authorship has been surpassed, the artist becomes a *collector* of communal production. This problematic has greater currency now than ever: most contemporary artists take the stage as compilers, analysts and 'remixers' of mass culture or media-industrial production. Even if they do not share the aesthetic of *Nouveau Réalisme*, Mike Kelley, John Miller, Jeremy Deller, Josephine Meckseper, Carol Bove and Sam Durant have followed in the footsteps of Raymond Hains and Jacques de la Villeglé; their artistic silhouette lends form to the mythical 'ragpicker' Baudelaire described: 'everything that the big city has thrown away, everything it has lost, everything it has scorned, everything it has crushed underfoot he catalogues and collects. He collates the annals of intemperance, the capharnaum of waste.'[34]

33 Benjamin Buchloh, *Essais historiques II* (Villeurbanne: Art édition, 1992), 44.

34 Quoted by Walter Benjamin, *Selected Writings: 1938–1940*, ed. Marcus Paul Bullock, Michael William Jennings (Cambridge: Harvard University Press, 2003), 48.

Like philosophy for Althusser, History for Benjamin represents a veritable *Kampfplatz*. That said, the battlefield has been scrupulously tidied by the victors. From where they now hold power, they have mastered the narrative of events. On the ground, or already buried, lies the debris of History, the *vanquished*; the latter are the concern of the materialist intellectual, who seeks out emblems and tools broken in defeat. The materialist historian endeavours to 'make present the totality of the past repressed by the vanquishers, just as the *flâneur* perceives a house that has been gutted more sharply than when, still intact, it formed part of his familiar landscape'.[35] In other words, one should write history by starting with scraps and ruins; the task is to reconstitute, patiently, a nomenclature of invisible buildings, to rediscover the exact form of the remnants on which the social edifice now stands. Above all, the 'historical rescue' Benjamin advocates settles a moral debt: revisiting the narrative of History means rendering justice to the vanquished lying in a mass grave teeming with half-erased accounts, embryonic futures and possible societies. In sketching this portrait of the 'materialist historian', Benjamin unintentionally described – but with astonishing precision – the relation to History that artists would adopt at the end of the twentieth and the beginning of the twenty-first centuries.

Writing as the threat of Nazi barbarism loomed, Benjamin viewed the proletariat and left-wing intellectuals as the exemplary *vanquished* of the age. Since then, postmodernists have scrupulously completed the list: in

35 Bruno Tackels, *Walter Benjamin. Une vie dans les textes* (Arles: Actes-sud, 2009), 626.

addition to the 'popular' classes, minorities – social, ethnic, sexual and political – are eligible for 'historical rescue', which will occur through unearthed documents attesting to the repression to which they are, or have been, subjected. The slightest clue, the meagrest fragment, can found new narratives: 'nothing that has ever happened should be regarded as lost for history'.[36] The 'materialist historian' picks up fallen memories in the form of *quotations*; for Benjamin, they are so many 'photographs' of the past – what we would now call 'readymades' or 'found objects'. Claude Lévi-Strauss described ethnology in the same terms: 'once while I was in the United States . . . I said that we were the ragpickers of history sifting through the garbage cans for our wealth.'[37] For all that, there is a difference between the anthropologist and the historian; even though they have the same object of research – social life – the one focuses on 'conscious expressions', whereas the other aims to 'find, behind observed practices, the unconscious mechanisms that govern them'.[38] Here, too, the unconscious marks a divide; interest bears on *what has been excluded*, the basis for a new science.

This lens permits one to analyze recent artistic developments, in particular works based on a critical rereading of the past through fragments and documents that qualify as 'historical' – provided that the designation also applies to what official history has cast off and the 'winners' do not wish to keep. Popular culture – alternatively, what is

36   Benjamin, *Illuminations*, 254.
37   Claude Lévi-Strauss and Didier Eribon, *Conversations with Lévi-Strauss*, trans. Paula Wissing (Chicago: University of Chicago Press, 1991), 122.
38   Ibid.

now called 'low culture' – has come to provide the artistic material of choice for the incipient twenty-first century. Such a development would be unthinkable without the Benjaminian theory of 'historical rescue': the political will to take on the sphere of ideology via the cultural hierarchies and official memory that it forges. That said, another element enters the equation, too – one tied to the very nature of the relationship between art and History. If one follows Benjamin's lead, History provides the stuff of art in a form that necessarily proves *accidental*. The 'photographs' of the past employed by the artist (and the 'materialist historian') belong either to the world of the 'conquered' – that is, they are mutilated or buried – or to the reigning ideological sphere. The full significance of the universe of the *dysfunctional* – rejected ideas, objects that have been cast off, and degraded ways of living – appears only to an aleatory vision of History affirming that everything *could have happened differently*. By the same token, other accidents may yet orient the world's march towards other 'suns' (as Stuart Hall puts it).

Since the late 1960s, Düsseldorf artist Hans Peter Feldmann has assembled small albums comprising found images, postcards, cuttings from newspapers or encyclopaedias, and publicity notices; occasionally, he includes his own photographs. These images – whether they present views from the window of his room or postcards of the Eiffel tower – are classified by a system whose logic is very personal, even esoteric. As a collector, if not a ragpicker, of iconography, Feldmann defies the simplistic efforts of classification that might tempt observers. To be sure, kinship exists between the images presented, but what is the principle organizing their presentation? What kind of archive is this? With Warburg, the logic of slippage and 'Chinese boxes' gained the right to take the intellectual stage. The logic of dreams – free association – holds. But far from staying confined to the psychic universe, as occurred in surrealism, the *evidential mode* now constitutes the privileged sociological approach for a somnambulistic art. Ryan Gander's *Loose Associations* – the title of a series of lectures – explores the ties between found images, projected one after the other. His work attests to the logic that has laid hold of the arts in general. Wolfgang Tillmans's *Truth Study Center* (an array of photographs and documents on tables) belongs in this context, too, as do the works of Aurélien Froment, Thomas Hirschhorn's sprawling object-environments, and Dominique Gonzalez-Foerster's memory theatres.

Through exaggerated iconographic contrasts, Josephine Meckseper stages confrontations between the glamour-universe that invaded the art world in the 2000s and the militancy of revolutionary avant-gardes that once fuelled its discourse – e.g., by juxtaposing a pamphlet calling for a strike and fashion photography. In her shelf-sculptures, Carol Bove brings together epochal documents (small objects, records, books . . .) to reconstitute the political, social and cultural constellation of American 'flower power'; Mai-Thu Perret takes up the same matter through the fiction of a 'feminist ranch' in an imaginary desert, where her works are supposed to come from. Then there are the investigations of historical figures undertaken by Kirsten Pieroth (Thomas Edison), Joachim Koester (Immanuel Kant, the explorer Salomon Andrée, Aleister Crowley, the *Club des haschishins* . . .) and Henrik Olesen (Alan Turing). Danh Vō engineers hybrid forms combining personal biography and macro-history. Walid Raad's project with the Atlas Group fabricates imaginary archives of an interminable war in Lebanon. Such works all attest to a drive to *produce* History – in the double sense of 'manufacture' and 'submit to (legal) judgment'.

Gardar Eide Einarsson has deconstructed the security ideology of the United States with bumper sticker slogans; in a series of video installations, Mark Leckey declares Felix the Cat the primitive fetish of the televisual age; Raphaël Zarka's works draw parallels between the history of the skateboard and Renaissance geometry; Cyprien Gaillard presents his work as archaeological 'digs' in twentieth-century civilization. All these artists rummage around in the dump of History to unearth buried material and reactive signals that have fallen into disuse: excavators of the minor, they present singular genealogies cutting through layers of history. Their use of materials points to History as a slow process of erosion; the present amounts to a heap of ruins, through which they reconstitute the architectural logic of the edifice that once stood. Books, everyday objects, visual motifs, and images from popular magazines are interrogated about the contexts to which they belonged – like the DNA samples a coroner uses to identify bodies. The formats artists employ freely refer to the scenography of History itself: now, at the beginning of the twenty-first century, display windows, shelves, libraries, *tableaux*, bits of popular museography and archaeological scaffolds have taken over exhibition spaces.

From the standpoint of the 'materialist historian', these artistic forms seem to stand outside of time. Nietzsche would have called them 'untimely'. Such *heterochrony* is the signature of our age. Artists enlist increasingly powerful computing tools to archive and research the most varied epochs and places, which they present simultaneously.

The aesthetic hallmark of this push towards intemporality is the widespread use of *black and white*. In films by Joachim Koester or Lindsay Seers – in the iconography of David Noonan, Tris Vonna-Mitchell, Mai-Thu Perret, Olivia Plender, Mario Garcia Torrés and Tacita Dean – the two-colour process provides a metaphor for the past; it signifies that the images on display belong to History. But at the same time, black-and-white refers to an ethical environment, a climate of authenticity, inasmuch as the images seem to come from a technological landscape that precedes digital manipulation and Photoshop. When it is produced on the scene of contemporary life and culture, black-and-white signals the aesthetics of *evidence*, cutting through historical and ideological falsifications. The fact that found objects occur in such formal diversity indicates that when quoting the past, contemporary art is less concerned with *readymades* – that is, with the definition of art – than with historical or political legitimacy. Artists as different as Danh Vô, Haris Epaminonda, Simon Fujiwara and Josephine Meckseper – whose works all exhume what has been cast away – occupy a position similar to Benjamin's, somewhere between the poet, the ragpicker and the historian. 'I needn't *say* anything. Merely show', Benjamin wrote; 'The rags, the refuse – these I will not inventory but allow, in the only way possible, to come into their own: by making use of them.'[39]

39   Walter Benjamin, *The Arcades Project*, trans. Howard Eiland and Kevin McLaughlin (Cambridge: Harvard University Press, 1999), 460.

When he spoke of *seeking justice* for the vanquished of History, Benjamin was invoking the Final Judgment – which underscores the messianic dimension of his thought. Pieces of evidence are produced before a tribunal because they serve as a clue or proof. 'The first will be the last' is another way of saying that even the least cultural maverick may find a central place in a narrative to come. Moreover, the pieces of evidence brought forth by contemporary artists attest to the 'materiality of ideology' that Althusser theorized; this occurs by way of an aesthetic that introduces fiction to archaeology, but which qualifies as *realist* inasmuch as it evinces the will to set the *real* of historical production in opposition to the prevailing ideology.

As acts of historical justice, quotations of the past appear in objective, factual and apparently documentary compositions – in order to insist on the potential of the fiction that elements reunited in this manner generate. Works of art tell us that every narrative of History belongs to the genre of the novel, just as Jorge Luis Borges declared philosophy a branch of fantastic literature. As such, artists identify symptoms of our present condition in the traces History has left behind. The new generation discerns the light, flashing with greater or lesser intensity, of the 'dialectical image' that signalled for Benjamin the transition between yesterday and today. 'It is not that what is past casts its light on what is present, or what is present its light on what is past,' he observed, 'rather, image is that wherein what has been comes together in a flash with the now to form a constellation.'[40]

40   Ibid., 463.

The Unconscious, Culture,
Ideology and Phantasmagoria

Phantasmagoria, ideology, culture and the unconscious represent four distinct formations corresponding to four levels of human existence. At the same time, they admit comparison in terms of a shared structural function: *expulsion*. Individual unconscious, community culture, societal ideology and civilizational phantasmagoria represent the unthought; one is subject to them, respectively, as a person, a member of a community, a citizen, and a subject of History. The individual assumes the destiny of being a subject via these four processes; as Althusser reminds us, subjectivity is a matter of 'membership' (*appartenance*). 'It is not by chance', he writes,

> that the subject designates one who is subjected, while according to its classical function in psychology, it designates one who is active. It is this reversal, for example, that constitutes the paradox of a psychology whose origin is manifestly political: the subject is one who submits to an order or to a master and who is at the same time thought in psychology to stand at the origin of his own actions.[41]

This amounts to saying goodbye to psychology, which Althusser defines as the mere 'by-product' of political, moral or philosophical ideology. Psychoanalysis, in contrast, stands on the side of philosophy, because both psychoanalysis and philosophy lay siege to what Althusser

41 Louis Althusser, *Psychanalyse et Sciences humaines. Deux conférences* (1963–64) (Paris: Livre de Poche, 1996), 107.

calls 'the ideological subject' – that is, the subject as 'the effect of structures anterior to its existence', the individual 'subjected to, or dominated by, ideological social relations'.[42] Everything takes place on the level of ideology, which provides 'the condition of individual existence'.[43]

As such, every subject stands exposed to four unmasterable swarms (*nuées*) producing dominant *norms* and *values*, whose hold on behaviour and thought cannot be fully compassed. Indeed, our unconscious is constituted in earliest infancy; our sensibility (*culture*) depends, to greater and lesser extents, on the identitarian context in which we mature; the ideology that suffuses us is transmitted by multiple 'ideological apparatuses'; finally, the 'phantasmagoria' in which we participate derives from the collective imaginary of our times. But for all that, it seems that the unconscious lies at the heart of this four-headed hydra, as its nucleus and prototype. Its tie to ideology is the central problem Althusser addressed – the concept at the core of his philosophy, no doubt. Ideology, he maintained, is where subjectivity is fabricated – once the 'savage' combat through which a child becomes a human being has ended. As individuals, we are transformed into social subjects because of what Althusser calls ideological 'interpellation', a process he compares to a police action:

> 'Hey, you there!' If . . . we suppose that the theoretical scene we are imagining happens in the street, the hailed individual turns around. With this simple 180-degree

42 Louis Althusser, *Sur la Philosophie* (Paris: Gallimard, 1994), 108.
43 Ibid., 75.

physical conversion, he becomes a *subject*. Why? Because he has recognized that the hail 'really' was addressed to him and that 'it really was he who was hailed' (not someone else).[44]

For Althusser, then, the subject emerges inasmuch as it is interpellated by ideology. On this score, one cannot fail to notice how analytic experience and, moreover, Lacan's influence prompted him to inject a good dose of Freudianism into Marxist studies. Althusser embraces the analogy between ideology and the unconscious (both of which operate 'behind our backs'): an individual is 'always already (a) subject', interpellated by ideology even before birth – as holds for the 'symbolic order' postulated by Lacan. Such 'ideological constraint and pre-appointment, and all the rituals of rearing and then education in the family, have some relationship with what Freud studie[d] in the forms of the pre-genital and genital "stages" of sexuality', Althusser observes in 'Ideology and Ideological State Apparatuses'.[45] More specifically: 'the human subject is decentered, constituted by a structure that, too, has a "center" solely in the imaginary misprision of the "ego," that is, in the ideological formations in which it "recognizes" itself'.[46]

In other words, the relationship between the individual and society duplicates, point for point, the relationship s/he entertains with his/her ego: ideology and the unconscious fatefully *decentre* the individual. One only seems

44 Louis Althusser, *On the Reproduction of Capitalism: Ideology and Ideological State Apparatuses*, trans. G. M. Goshgarian (London: Verso, 2014), 191.
45 Althusser, *Lenin and Philosophy*, 176.
46 Althusser, *Writings on Psychoanalysis*, 31.

to be one's own master – in fact, one is constructed through blows of interpellation from outside. Thus, if analysis aims to recentre the subject by rewriting the personal scenario in which it is caught, a comparable effort should be made with respect to the social scenario, i.e., work enabling us not to respond mechanically to ideological *interpellation*. The definition Althusser provides corresponds to this double exigency. On the one hand, 'ideology is a "representation" of the imaginary relationship of individuals to their real conditions of existence'.[47] On the other hand, he describes it as inherently repressive: 'ideology has the function of assuring the *bond* among people in the totality of the forms of their existence, the *relation* of individuals to their tasks assigned by the social structure'.[48] In this way, he demonstrates that the subject is produced by intersubjectivity; and because it results from exterior 'interpellation' fashioned by interhuman relations, it is *political* in essence.

These reflections will no doubt surprise those who think that our epoch has settled such matters. But in this instance, the cliché about the 'end of ideologies' turns out to be purely ideological itself. Such an illusion is readily explained by confusion about ideology's true nature: ideology is not a matter of any 'content' in particular; rather, it is a relationship between human beings, more specifically, a relation of *subjugation* that seems to be freely accepted, a sentiment of membership or belonging.

Althusser invokes Blaise Pascal to bolster his theory of ideological state apparatuses. 'Pascal says more or less:

47   Althusser, *Lenin and Philosophy*, 162.
48   Quoted in Rancière, *Althusser's Lesson*, 130.

"Kneel down, move your lips in prayer, and you will believe".[49] In other words, *practice* produces belief, and ideology rests on actions and structures. Why does this insistence on the material character of ideology seem so singular today? Because we have slowly come to accept a massive devaluation of thinking; more specifically, thought has become completely disconnected from action. The reigning ideology proceeds by stealth, radically separating *what can be thought* from *what can be done*. This 'cut' insinuates that no *serious* connection holds between ethics and practice, between ideas and the real. Positing a relationship between abstract speculation and concrete action amounts to a scandalous pretension branded as *naïve* – unless it finds support in the ultimate ideological state apparatus recognized as the official alternative: religion. Reducing the array of positions to a binary opposition between the religious and the secular, 'fanatics' and pragmatists, perfectly suits the programme of capitalist ideology. Indeed, it works so well that the average politician has become a man of action priding himself in having 'his feet on the ground' and eschewing 'dogmatism' of any kind. It now counts as self-evident that the economic sphere cannot harbour the slightest trace of ideology; because it is efficient by nature, we are told it has no other purpose.

Thus, the 'everything is political' of Althusser's times has given way, in just a few decades, to the following syllogism: 'everything is economic' – that is, pragmatic, or natural. Yet as strange as it may now seem, pragmatism is nothing but ideology. As Žižek stresses, 'To say that good ideas are "ideas that work" means that one

49 Althusser, *Lenin and Philosophy*, 166.

accepts in advance the (global capitalist) constellation which determines what works.'[50] From this point on, the act of thinking implies keeping distant from politics and economics – renouncing efforts to achieve a concrete effect on the world as it stands. Specific spaces are set aside for this kind of speculation; their connection to the sphere of action is stretched further every day; alternatively, they are reorganized at the behest of power: the *expert* is the figure embodying collaboration of this sort. In a word, in order to preserve the capitalist system of production, ideas must be relegated to a field where they have only display value – without any relation to economic or political reality. It is striking that contemporary art has been contaminated by this call for efficiency. Haunted by its inability to think about the way things are, it evinces boundless nostalgia for modernism: a discourse calling for ideas and action, criticism and engagement. Indeed, we would be at great pains to *quantify* the effects of art on society. According to the prevailing ideology of 'pragmatism', which recognizes only numbers and tangible effects, this is enough to disqualify art's political pretensions. Art, the very site where ideology is laid bare, has become the space where politics is deployed, where it becomes a matter of *display value*, pure and simple. The positions artists take are all the more extreme because no one believes that they can have the slightest effect on the real, which is cemented by ideology.

Whether on the street or in our homes, advertising and economic information *interpellate* us directly as subjects of capitalist ideology – that is, as consumers. This

50 Slavoj Žižek, *The Ticklish Subject: The Absent Centre of Political Ontology* (London: Verso, 1999), 199.

discourse defines us, day after day, as the subjects of an imaginary realm based on acquisition, the salariat; here, money is the motor of all action. It would be mistaken to think the art world has escaped this effect of interpellation. To be sure, the work of art is not addressed to consumers – at least not *a priori* . . . Indeed, if the term refers to individuals who actually *buy* works of art, there are few consumers. That said, consumption (as an ideology) does not stop at the concrete act of purchasing: observers, even if they do not possess the financial means to acquire a work of art, play the part of passive spectators of others' sumptuary consumption. In turn, if public art interpellates *empty* individuals – that is, parties free to understand themselves as subjects of the *polis* (citizens), members of a given community, or art lovers – it winds up being determined by its position within a society ruled by an ideology of consumption applied to the urban environment. Alain Badiou reminds us that such contempt for thinking was not always a matter of course: 'In Althusser's view, the origin of the great historical failures of the proletariat lay not in the crude balance of power, but in theoretical deviations . . . That weakness is always, in the last analysis, an intellectual weakness.'[51]

Karl Marx and Walter Benjamin both used the term *phantasmagoria* to describe the essence of the capitalist economy. The former did so in speaking of the 'fetish character of the commodity'. The commodity, he explained, has transformed into an idol that, even though it is the product of human hands, dictates its own rules to people. This fetishization of commodities stems from the

---

51   Alain Badiou, *Pocket Pantheon: Figures of Postwar Philosophy*, trans. David Macey (London: Verso, 2009), 55.

capitalist system of labour: a social relation takes on, in the eyes of those who inhabit it, the fantastic form of a relation between things. As such, phantasmagoria, like ideology, comprises 'imaginary representations' that exercise a powerful effect on human behaviour. They possess the same characteristics as the unconscious, and they act in the same way. For all that, the unconscious does not have the same nature as what is called *an* imaginary: it is composed of linguistic debris, buried memories, traces. As such, it stands related to a universe of ruins, and the social edifice – like our personalities – is founded on these ruins. In the analytic cure, an individual's relation to his or her unconscious prompts a quest similar to the philosopher's effort to disclose ideology under the surface of things or facts, the artist's incorporation of documents or debris from the past into compositions, and, finally, the method employed by Benjamin's 'materialist historian'. Ideology, Althusser explains, is not 'an idea that is the fruit of individual fancy'; rather, it comes 'from a system of notions that can be socially projected'.[52] In other words, ideology is a kind of film, analogous to phantasmagoria.

What fascinated Benjamin about Marx above all was this notion of phantasmagoria: the fact that reified inter-human relations emerge from the fetishizing idealization of commodities – that is, from a kind of collective dream. Because monetary relations between commodities dictate relations between human beings, phantasmagoria transforms subjects into objects; conversely, it turns commodities into self-sufficient subjects. In this context, Marx speaks of a 'spectral dance': things come alive,

52   Althusser, *Sur la philosophie*, 69.

and human beings stop being anything more than ghosts of themselves. We shouldn't forget that, etymologically, *phantasmagoria* means 'to make ghosts speak in public'. Accordingly, it is no accident that Benjamin uses the same word – which simultaneously designates the fetishism of value and a magic show (*spectacle féérique*). For him, the 'phantoscope' – the projection device used in the first phantasmagoric *séances* at the end of the eighteenth century – is Capital itself. Capital distances us, through the fictions it offers, from what underlies our objective existence in concrete terms, and it drags us towards an existence as ghostly as that of the products surrounding us. Inasmuch as it inverts the terms of subject and object, concrete and abstract, phantasmagoria represents the essential pivot linking what Marxist theory calls 'base' and 'superstructure' – the everyday life the individual lives and the collective dream that carries him or her along. Ideology, which Althusser defines as a system that must be socially 'projected', constitutes a phantasmagoria through and through – and *ideological state apparatuses* are so many phantascopes for its diffusion.

Benjamin sought to reconstruct the phantasmagoria specific to the nineteenth century by studying the streets and boulevards of Paris in detail. Commercial arcades, the system of public lighting, the decor of bourgeois interiors, and objects displayed at universal expositions represent enigmatic features of a building in ruins – strips of film on the cutting room floor. For Benjamin, dreams do not stand in opposition to the spirit of historical materialism; instead, they constitute its raw material. At the same time, however, the true sense of a given historical moment – that is, the significance of a collective dream

– is apparent only at the moment of waking. The historian seeks to wrest scraps of meaning from what sleep has left behind; he is a ragpicker rummaging in piles of ruins, attempting to reconstitute the past mentally by accumulating *details* gleaned here and there. Initially, the crumbled edifice offers a mass of incomprehensible fragments; they reveal their meaning only after the fact, following patient decipherment, once the phantasmagoria to which they belong has vanished.

Between 1968 and 1972, Belgian artist Marcel Broodthaers devoted himself to an elaborate project: *Museum of Modern Art, Department of Eagles*. In this series of works, fiction became a medium in its own right. Starting with his first exhibition in 1964, Broodthaers crafted magisterial works centred on the notion of reification – notably, a series of paintings consisting of a mass of mussels (*moules*) evoking industrial production by *moulding* (*moulage*). His attention then shifted to the Museum as a totalizing form, the central site of cultural commodification. Here, the signs that artists bring into circulation transform into economic and cultic quantities, as well as historical documents. Broodthaers decided to use this *found format* as a readymade and developed, in twelve sequences, the fiction of a Museum without a fixed location. In his work, the figure of the 'Eagle' functions as a substitute for art. The majestic flying creature becomes the emblem of a complex fiction exploring the formal and ideological universe of cultural reification comprising various 'sections': *Section cinéma, section des figures, section documentaire, services financiers, réserves ...* 'My system of inscription', Broodthaers declared, invites observers to 'separate, in an object, what is art and what is ideological. I want to show ideology as it is, and precisely to prevent art from making this ideology inapparent, that is, effective.'[53]

Every epoch produces a specific form of phantasmagoria. How is this not ideology? The difference appears when one employs the tools Benjamin and Althusser developed to illuminate each one in particular. The former, the ragpicker of History, reconstituted the phantasmagoria of nineteenth-century France by examining details or detached pieces; Althusser, in turn, dismantled the ideology of the present by starting with massive objects: *ideological state apparatuses*. To state matters summarily, phantasmagoria is a matter of culture, and ideology a matter of politics – even though these categories intersect at more than one point, and even though they both entertain a murky relationship to fiction. Without collective narratives to feed them, they languish. They both speak 'behind our backs', as Althusser puts it. Like dreams, they both have the power to pass themselves off as true. Contemporary art, however, approaches ideology by way of its concrete effects – that is, via the *norm*: the ensemble of cultural, social and political conventions and *obvious facts* (*évidences*) structuring daily life. In committing themselves to the analysis or disruption of (seeming) logic, artists take a position – sometimes without knowing as much – within the *realist project* inaugurated by Gustave Courbet. Such realism does not involve seeking points of resemblance with reality; rather, it refutes established norms in the name of an *Ideal* – thereby bringing mechanisms of expulsion to light. It may be defined with the pointed words Althusser

---

53   Conversation with Georges Adé, 1972, in *Marcel Broodthaers* (Paris: Galerie Nationale du Jeu de Paume, 1992).

used to explain materialism: *not to indulge in storytelling* – and especially where the domain of dreams is concerned. In other words, it means taking ideology, phantasmagoria and the unconscious of the times head-on – confronting the *Angel of the Masses*.

III
The Realist Project

The early 2000s witnessed the advent of Google, which promoted aleatory information searches; its associative logic achieved such dominance that other types of human activity became contaminated. Then, Web 2.0 entered the scene, along with social networks such as MySpace, Facebook, YouTube and Tumblr, which all represent the drive to document and archive even the least gestures of everyday life – anything at all that an individual might experience is placed within reach of everyone else. Today, documentation professionals must devise veritable screenplays, because *reality is documented by all, not by one*. If photography accompanied the colonialist ambition of showing the faraway and bringing it back to Western metropolises in authentic form, Web 2.0 sounded the death knell for the ethnographic drive which animated the nineteenth century. Now, every group-subject – and on a planetary scale – can directly attest to the real of its experience by immediately producing objects and documents reflecting it in detail. This distinction between reality and the real corresponds to what separates optical realism (which may be called 'verism'), or art that aims to *expose (a) reality*, from a wholly different pursuit that may be traced back to the aesthetic position taken by Gustave Courbet.

Reality is the phenomenal world inasmuch as it offers a support for representation; here, we live as subjects of ideology, in a mode of membership/belonging and subjugation. The real, in contrast, may be defined as this same phenomenal world, but freed from ideology and idealizing impulses. What will be described in the following as artistic *realism*, then, has nothing to do with artists' ability to depict a reality that is visible or intelligible. It must not be confused with the documentary format, or genre, that has passed for providing the *nec plus ultra* in restoring/reproducing reality since the end of the twentieth century. The Real is another matter altogether … Equally, such realism exceeds the narrow frame of twentieth-century pictorial realisms that, alas, have claimed the title for their own projects.

Courbet and the Big Toe

In 1855, Gustave Courbet exhibited his works outside the official salon, in a 'Pavilion of Realism' he had had built to this end. A huge painting captured general attention, in part because of its title: *The Artist's Studio: A Real Allegory for a Seven-year Phase of My Artistic Life*. The canvas does not represent a workplace so much as a space-and-time of production; according to its creator, it depicts 'the moral and physical history of my atelier'.[1]

---

1   Catherine Strasser, *Le Temps de la production* (Strasbourg: École des arts décoratifs, 1997), 17.

On the right, a small crowd of characters surrounds the painter, who is busy working on a landscape; these are his 'shareholders, by which I mean friends, workers, and art lovers'. On the left stands social reality, represented by personages Courbet had encountered at one point or another. We should note that each of these figures was inspired by a person who really existed, instead of merely representing a *type*. There is no abstraction in Courbet's painting; each figure is singular. Likewise, metal, stone, wood, fur, water and foliage – matter in general – is always rendered with utmost care.

Stressing the artist's contemporaneity with the invention of photography, Youssef Ishaghpour has advanced a convincing hypothesis about the attention paid to different surfaces and textures:

> Courbet is situated precisely at the moment when art detaches from imitation of the idea, form and antiquity – when the very existence of photography marks their end – and must affirm the materiality of nature, not by reproducing it (wherein it differs from photography) but through the proximity and identity of its own pictorial power to nature.[2]

The fundamental difference between these two 'realisms', Ishaghpour continues, stems from the fact that 'photography presents the trace, the effect, and the realm of light, whereas Courbet's painting proceeds as the unfolding of matter'.[3] In consequence, we should not view such

---

2   Youssef Ishaghpour, *Courbet. Le Portrait de l'artiste dans son atelier* (Strasbourg: Circé, 2011), 70.

3   Ibid., 99.

realism as a mere depiction of how the poorer classes live; nor should it be viewed as visual propaganda of socialist inspiration. Courbet's political project does not lie here. To be sure, as Linda Nochlin observes, *L'Atelier* is an allegory portraying 'the Fourierist ideal of the Association of Capital, of Labor, and of Talent',[4] and Courbet certainly meant to paint the world he inhabited *politically*. Still, it is not just a matter of presenting left-wing symbolism – which would amount simply to setting one ideal against another. What is more, this rejection of the 'painted idea' provoked a disagreement tainting his amicable relations with Proudhon: the theorist of anarchism – although very attached to Courbet – hardly understood what was at stake in his pictures. Proudhon held that art should seek to capture 'what is True' and, to be sure, 'the Idea'; it should be critical and edifying. 'Art is nothing except through the Ideal; it has no value but for the Ideal', he wrote.[5] How many of his contemporaries also failed to see art in terms other than 'content' and ideal value?

If the realist movement, of which Courbet declared himself the leader, did not pursue an Idea, it also did not seek mere resemblance; instead, the aim was a *direct pictorial relation to the real as it is lived*. In the artist's own words, the goal is 'aesthetics founded on action, engagement, and the capacity for transformation':[6] in other words, it stands at a vast remove from what would come to be called *realist* art in the following century. In

4   Linda Nochlin, *The Politics of Vision: Essays on Nineteenth-century Art and Society* (Boulder: Westview Press, 1991), 10.

5   Emile Zola, Pierre-Joseph Proudhon, *Controverse sur Courbet et l'utilité sociale de l'art* (Paris: 1001 Nuits), 47

6   Strasser, *Le Temps de la production*, 26.

shorthand, it is closer to a Joseph Beuys than to a Lucian Freud. Courbet already voiced the modernist demand that adequation between art and the state of the world be achieved through 'objective' ways of transferring painting onto a support – a mode of production *contemporaneous* with the prevailing economic and political system.

From Malevich to Jackson Pollock, Ed Ruscha and Frank Stella, modernist painters were obsessed with establishing a compelling relationship between their practice and their times. This prompted them to explore the *real* instead of validating official narratives. Such is the realism at issue: to open, by formal means, a path outside of ideology (that is, outside of all idealism), whereby the artist enters into dialogue with the world as it is, from a standpoint as close as possible to its historical, political and social materiality. 'Historical art', Courbet explained, 'is by nature contemporary.'[7] In other words: our vision of the past is not primarily a relation to the ideology of the present; being realistic – which is synonymous with *contemporary* for Courbet – means devising a channel connecting artistic practice and the *real* of one's historical context. Whether such practices are 'figural' or 'abstract' does not matter.

Courbet developed the idea at the Antwerp Congress in 1861: 'Through my affirmation of the negation of the ideal and all that springs from the ideal I have arrived at the emancipation of the individual and finally at democracy. Realism is essentially the democratic art.'[8] 'Democratic' ambition begins with refusing the traditional hierarchy governing genres and subjects; above all,

7 Ishaghpour, *Courbet*, 25–6.
8 Ibid., 104.

however, it means refusing to idealize or ennoble reality as perceived along the uniform lines dictated by power. The 'negation of the ideal' undertaken by Courbet, which provides the theoretical key to his realism, occurs by affirming pictorial matter and representing beings and things such as they are – that is, outside the role the reigning ideology assigns them. Courbet sensed that the 'Ideal' – on which academic painters and Proudhonian anarchists agreed, even if they differed on matters of content – conceals an ideological machine serving to legitimate preconstituted political representations. His paintings do not draw their force from his willingness to depict labourers breaking rocks or sharpening tools in the same way that kings or aristocrats were represented at the time. His art is revolutionary in its capacity for dismantling the ideology that orders their symbolic position – as in *L'Atelier*, which reorganizes social life in terms of the painter's 'real' instead of aligning it with verisimilitude or a *respectable* narrative. Another manifesto of realism, *The Origin of the World*, declared war on the ideal of the classical 'nude' by showing what might well constitute its 'real': a vagina unaccompanied by any narrative, unadorned by a mythological pretext, literary reference, or content exterior to itself.

Inasmuch as ideology, according to Althusser, 'function[s] . . . to ensure the cohesion of the social whole by regulating the relations of all individuals to their tasks',[9] the ideology governing the aesthetic in Courbet's day determined painters' relationship to their subject matter. His paintings provoked scandal because they

9   Quoted in Jacques Rancière, *Althusser's Lesson*, trans. Emiliano Battista (London: Bloomsbury, 2011), 130.

revealed the gap between the real and the ideal, between matter and ideology. In a word, Courbet's art does not 'indulge in storytelling' – which is how Althusser defines materialism. In turn, Édouard Manet experienced the same rejection with his *Luncheon on the Grass*: inasmuch as the ideological basis legitimating the painting had been removed, history and myth expelled, and the idea of the 'pastoral concerto' banished, the public could no longer see anything but two students in the company of women of ill repute. Manet reduced ideology, which speaks *behind the public's back*, to silence: the only remaining option was to take offence at its prosaic *reality* in order to avoid exposure to the *Real* of the painting. *Olympia* met with a comparable outcry. Hans Belting perceptively observes:

> Manet put on view not only the real body but the actual painting. This is a confusing double strategy that invites the following conclusion. Just as the woman sells herself in the boudoir, so the painter sells himself in the Salon, for his picture too has a price and lays itself bare before a buyer.[10]

The collective blindness provoked by modern painting, the dogged refusal to see painting for what it is (that is, according to Maurice Denis's famous definition, 'shapes and colours arranged in a certain order'), amounts to the denial of commerce, a veil of modesty cast over the market value and material reality of art. Such realism, to use Georges Bataille's expression, 'twists the neck of eloquence' and all idealizing rhetoric: it dispels thick

10   Hans Belting, *The Invisible Masterpiece*, trans. Helen Atkins (Chicago: University of Chicago Press, 2001), 170.

clouds of ideology by making breaches through which the *Real* bursts in.

From the inception, modern art's destiny has been tied to *déclassement*. First of all, this concerns the subject: the will to depict modern life instead of rooting around in the mythological, historical and edifying repertoire that once authorized painters to represent the world. Second, it concerns trades (*métier*): the public perceived the 'unfinished' quality of impressionist canvases as a double affront to artisanal craftsmanship and industrial objects. The visible presence of the painter's hand – brushstrokes – was all it took to plunge modern art into the universe of refuse and cast-offs. Expelled from the collective phantasmagoria, such 'trash' developed into a *supplementary world* where the objects that society devalues or rejects can be redeemed and transfigured by artistic intervention. The Impressionists' suburban views, African masks collected by Derain, Matisse or Picasso, industrial objects to which Marcel Duchamp lent a 'new idea', the bicycle seat and handlebars that Picasso made into his *Bull's Head* in 1943, and the supermarket packaging of pop artists share the feature of being *without value* as subject matter until the artist intervenes and transfigures them.

The history of modern art is summed up by the progressive splitting of natural Beauty and artistic Beauty, abandoning the ideal sphere where grandeur and the sublime had evolved, and embracing the 'anything at all' that came along and furnished a subject and raw material. At least in part: between Marcel Duchamp and Kazimir Malevich – between the sceptical, materialist path and the road taken by pictorial metaphysics – a gulf emerged, and two distinct artistic families were created. Two other figures also embody these two sides of the debate: Georges Bataille and André Breton.

In response to the latter, in whom he saw the epitome of surrealist idealism, Bataille invented the concept of *heterology*, 'the science of what is completely other'.[11] At the time, Bataille hesitated between this term and *agiology*, even *scatology*, for he meant to found a *'science of excrement [ordure]'* that would explore the excremental dimension of man and the universe. Ultimately, he chose the term *hetero* ('entirely other') to designate what resists all homogenizing efforts. Bataille defined heterology as 'what opposes any homogeneous representation of the world, in other words, any philosophical system'.[12] It is the domain of the inappropriable, of what escapes 'all possible common measure' and defies all transcendence: in a word, it is a war machine against idealism, launched at the 'wondrous' the surrealists held so dear. The big toe wading in the mud assaults the body's nobler parts. An avid reader of Hegel, Bataille sought out what cannot provide the object of synthesis, what resists all 'sublation' (*Aufhebung*).

As Bataille viewed matters, every thought produces a residue – an element that remains unclassifiable within the finite chain of propositions constituting a theory. Every methodological form of appropriation (whether it involves labour or knowledge) frees up a 'heterogeneous excremental object'.[13] He meant to base his thinking on the inassimilable, all that has been cast off. In other

---

11 Georges Bataille, *Oeuvres complètes*, Volume II (Paris: Gallimard, 1973), 61.
12 Ibid., 62.
13 Ibid., 63.

words, his thought is founded on the *excluded*, and its theoretical objects come from the sphere of the socially inappropriable: eroticism, luxury, waste, potlatch, the abject, the sacred. There is no 'Idea' of waste in Plato, nor could there be. Bataille, in contrast, wanted to account for epistemological refuse and to delimit the domain of the *unmanageable*. His project, then, concerns the science of the limits inherent in all processes of appropriation; it sets into relief the movement of expulsion that occurs in the formation of all knowledge. In a word, it offers a 'theory of the tension between the homogeneous world and what finds no place in it [*ne s'y résorbe pas*]'.[14]

Bataille's anti-idealism centres on a profound reflection on the *sphere of the useful* and labour, understood as a tool for cutting up and dividing reality. Here, nature is put in the service of productive ends – first by making something the object of exchange, and, ultimately, through activity that yields sums of information. Labour segments reality infinitely. It is always subordinate to an end, organized in view of a final state. Bataille's effort to theorize *uselessness* proves all the more timely for clearly identifying an immense domain of reality that, before him, had never been taken into account as such. He demonstrated that all thinking remains tainted by idealism if it fails to account for refuse and loss, religious ecstasy and erotic pleasure, tears and bodily fluxes. The ludic, eroticism, mysticism and art all connect to sumptuary waste, which proves irreducible to the 'sphere of the useful'. Human activity does not necessarily have any 'gain' at its horizon; it may refuse to put itself in the

14   Robert Sasso, *Georges Bataille, le système du non-savoir. Une ontologie du jeu* (Paris: Editions de Minuit, 1978).

service of a purpose. For Bataille, the first economic principle is not the accumulation of goods, but *potlatch* – the name for the ritual in which certain Native American tribes compete to destroy their most luxurious possessions. Such is the 'accursed share' of the human economy: this practice of 'loss' cannot be boiled down to the binary of production and consumption; it borders on the irrational and means placing one's very life at risk. In this sphere, Bataille includes 'luxury, mourning, war, worship, games, spectacles, art, perverse sexuality (i.e., not for reproductive purposes) . . .'.

Since the mid-nineteenth century, artistic modernity has taken form around the central division between the useful and the useless. Essentially, this has occurred in opposition to the dictates of the former, fighting to preserve a *poetic* zone within a functionalist world. Sometimes, however, it has identified with the forms and principles of this world – as when the Bauhaus or Russian constructivists integrated general production into everyday decors. At any rate, the presence of art in a given society, its recognition by operative ideological and institutional apparatuses, depends on local inflections of this problematic of utility, which traces a line of demarcation between the *product*, which is socially useful, and *waste*, which is supposed to be rejected and held at a distance. This line, invisible yet active on all levels of social organization, draws the contours of a shifting zone whose borders are ceaselessly crossed in both directions: *waste* represents a temporary category – one that is largely arbitrary and prone to infinite renegotiation. In the intellectual domain, as we have seen, cultural studies has set up shop on the traces of this line of division. An airlock, as it were, between the realms of the exalted and the paltry, the valuable and the worthless, it recycles and constantly questions the validity of judgements that have consigned a given item to the dump.

The problematic of waste has become central to socio-economic life – and to such an extent that a new field of study has been devoted to it: *rudology*. Derived from the Latin *rudus* ('rubble'), this science deems waste an object of analysis enabling one to understand the economic sphere and social practices by focusing on processes of *devalorization* generated by human activity, as well as reprocessing technologies. Rudology examines social facts starting with marginal traces; as such, it rejoins Bataille's method of exploring the depths of collective psychology and Benjamin's efforts to reconstitute the ideological cathedral of the nineteenth century by way of scattered fragments gathered in the Parisian arcades.

Among twentieth-century art movements – at least before the Situationist International – surrealism certainly offered the aesthetic project with the greatest theoretical virulence against the reign of the useful (Bataille's criticisms notwithstanding). The surrealist *oeuvre* – although the very term was redolent of labour and money for artists – presents itself as a residue of oneiric activity, that is, as coming from a spiritual regime that resists any and all social recuperation. The surrealist irrational represents a declaration of war on the practical world and Reason, which it consigns to the camp of drudgery and toil. On this score, the movement led by André Breton acknowl-edged its debt to Dadaism. At the same time, it added a wilfully nostalgic iconography deliberately turned towards the remains of the past – fed by frequent excur-sions to the flea markets at the gates of Paris. Accordingly, the *obsolete* represents the main ferment for the wonder the surrealists prized, as Benjamin stressed. Needless to say, he appreciated their interest in outmoded trinkets, illustrations of the fashions of the past, and dusty boutiques. In turn, the Situationist International – which found support for its theories in comic books and kung-fu films – conferred titles of political nobility on 'low culture': if artistic forms are alienated, their effects can only be simulated by *détournement* of popular images that do not bother to hide the fact that they reflect the dominant ideology. In this, both the surrealists and the Situationists were the direct descendents of the realism inaugurated by Courbet, who never failed to draw inspiration from the popular productions of his day – e.g., almanacs, engravings, and songs.[15]

Art, Labour and Waste

Since Courbet, relations between the artist and the universe of labour have shaped the evolution of art – as has the relationship between art and waste. Art has always been 'informed' by the system of production, but artistic modernity such as it appeared at the end of the nineteenth century demanded that the relationship be problematized pictorially: spurred by the competition offered by photography, art found itself demoted to a mere *supplement* – if not to a socially obsolete activity. Starting from here, one can understand the projects of modernist painters from Strzemiński to Ed Ruscha, whose

15 Meyer Schapiro, 'Courbet and Popular Imagery: An Essay on Realism and Naïveté', *Journal of the Warburg and Courtauld Institutes* 4: 3/4 (1941–42): 164–91.

pictorial practices sought objective means to transfer coloured matter from the paint tube to the canvas. Hereby, 'objective' means 'suited to a logic of production calibrated on production in general' – methods *contemporary* with the economic system and structures in which they have evolved. In other words, artists have responded to the specific questions that arose in their times or reformulated older questions by means of the tools at their disposal.

From the second half of the nineteenth century on, art has constantly problematized its relationship with social production, whether by endorsing 'art for art's sake' or by making peace with the system of production in one way or another. At one end of the landscape, Andy Warhol teamed up with the industrial universe by openly identifying himself with a 'machine', specifically, the camera. At the other end, Robert Filliou sought to be the citizen of a great '*république géniale*' made up of idle and contemplative 'bistro geniuses'. Whatever the position – from frontal opposition to a mimetic bearing – it is determined by an equation dating from the inception of modernity: art, expelled from the social body, or threatened by this fate, has constituted a mere appendix of society, a supplement of the system of production whose legitimacy always stands in doubt. In an ornamental or unproductive capacity, art turns into an oxygen tank for a functionalist system; by pretending to be socially useful or to belong to a democratic ontology, it seeks to make its necessity felt by clinging as closely as possible to processes of production and debates within the community.

In 1964, the *Service Technique provincial* of Liège, Belgium, hired Jacques Charlier. He was joined by one André Bertrand, who had the job of conducting photographic surveys to assess the state of the municipality's public works. In an artistic capacity, Charlier took these pictures 'out of context', along with other documents – attendance registers, groups portraits of administrators, and dossiers – and made them the raw material of his exhibitions. The series of black-and-white photographs he assembled in vast, rectangular displays is called *Professional Landscapes*. They show trenches dug for pipes, details of roadwork, and abandoned intersections . . . The observer senses allusions to the works of Bernd and Hilla Becher, who, from 1959 on, systematically documented (through frames at fixed intervals and photographs in black and white) industrial architecture, blast furnaces and water towers. Charlier, however, was critical of their enterprise. The Bechers, in his eyes, effaced political reality through overly 'aestheticizing' presentation. The constructions they photographed, he explained, are neither sculptural nor 'anonymous': 'They are, after all, industrial facilities made by construction workers, . . . designed by engineers, . . . owned by factory bosses. All these people have a name, . . . a story. Concealing them . . . is part of the usual process of artistic appropriation.'[16] As Charlier was pursuing his project, Joseph Beuys made the same argument about artistic appropriation as *expropriation* apropos of Marcel Duchamp's urinal: the worker who dug up the kaolin used to manufacture it was every bit as much a 'creator' as the person who came along, signed it, and put it on display. Both performed a 'putting-into-form' (*Gestaltung*) that 'acts on all the fields of forces within society and all

16   Jacques Charlier, *Dans les règles de l'art* (Brussels: Lebeer Hossmann, 1983), 43.

contexts of labour'.[17] Like Beuys, Charlier insisted on the artist's duty not to conceal the process of production or isolate the object aesthetically – in other words, to view himself within a greater system of production, not above it or standing on the sidelines.

Thirty years later, in 1993, Maurizio Cattelan exhibited a piece entitled *Lavorare è un brutto mestiere* ('Work Is a Dirty Job') at the Venice Biennale. The artist rented the space to an advertising agency, which then used it for one of its campaigns. Cattelan's gesture exemplifies how the artist's relationship to the working world has changed from top to bottom. He or she has become one 'professional' among others, ready to enlist different trades; the artist has abandoned, if nothing else, any *symbolic* claim that s/he is revealing structures of production in exchange for a kind of realism (verging on cynicism in this case) that inserts his/her work into the ordinary flux of production. In other words, the world of labour (workers, factories . . .) no longer constitutes an outer symbolic referent for artistic practice, as held for the avant-gardes of the 1960s and '70s: henceforth, it forms the substrate of a post-Fordist mental space governed by the binary salary/capital, which has been diverted from context, as it were.

Cattelan presents the artist as the symbolic occupant of an *exhibition space* from which an income may be drawn. The system of production itself finds use as a readymade. The worker is transformed into a *proletarian* through the passage from the world of being to that of having: under capitalism, labour power, which constitutes a source of free energy *a priori*, becomes an item of exchange. When Joseph

17 Joseph Beuys, *Par la présente, je n'appartiens plus au monde de l'art* (Paris: L'Arche, 1988), 59.

Beuys declared that everyone is an artist, he voiced a magi-
cal equation that materialized the objectives of Marxism in
the here and now: a classless society where everyone is in
the position to realize his or her human essence. In contrast,
when Maurizio Cattelan illegally sublets his exhibition
space, he traces a connection between the artist and the
undocumented immigrant – one without either 'being' or
'having', who survives by seizing the *chances* life offers.
This is the very essence of Cattelan's work: to exploit
opportunity, to constitute a purely opportunistic aesthetic.
In turn, artists from Africa such as George Adéagbo or El
Anatsui, when they recycle old newspapers or bottle caps,
offer a response to Cattelan's sarcastic praise of 'bare life'
from the point of view of garbage collectors . . .

In Courbet, but still more explicitly in Georges Seurat,
one can already see the opposition labour/leisure: *Sunday*
stands as a figure for what the working week, its complic-
itous counterpart, has left over. The mechanical stiffness
of the people strolling in *A Sunday Afternoon on the
Island of La Grande Jatte* (1883) inaugurated the theme
of dehumanized leisure. Here, the Parisian suburb takes
on the aspect of a vast no-man's-land where it seems that
machines are performing gestures of rest and amusement:
Seurat was painting the crowds at the amusement parks
in the course of emerging. More than a century later,
John Miller took a series of untitled photographs, all made
between noon and two o'clock, during the lunch break.
Reversing Jacques Charlier's gesture in *Paysages profes-
sionnels*, Miller showed that 'time off' is now a compo-
nent of the working world, which alone lends it meaning.
Free time belongs to the universe of what production has
discarded – except when it can be channelled towards
leisure that generates new profits. All that remains, then,

is the switch between 'on' and 'off' in time entirely devoted to the returns of capital. Today, the proletarian is defined as the consumer-of-the-world, pure and simple; his original patch of land – which Fordist-era factories provided so that he would employ free time in a useful manner – has assumed the immense dimensions of the 'world of leisure'. For all that, however, the concept invented by nineteenth-century industry has not really changed: more than ever, free time remains indexed to the world of work. *Entertainment* represents the logical continuation of employment for pay – which is evident in capitalism's horror at unproductive waste. In other words, the postmodern notion of leisure, conceived as a supplement to working life, simply prolongs work – just as recycling extends industrial production by recreating value at the very heart of a wasteland.

In 1995, Pierre Huyghe founded *L'Association des temps libérés*, the theoretical prelude to his exploration of leisure as a concrete force. The same year, Philippe Parreno presented the installation *Werktische*: he asked ten people to come and pursue their favourite hobbies on Labour Day. Rirkrit Tiravanija, in turn, has encouraged visitors at expositions to sit at a table and share a meal. Do these daily activities amount to work, then, or leisure – or do they dissolve into a spectacle?

A series of pieces by John Miller, executed between 1990 and 1993, comprises cheap junk – plastic toys, gadgets and worthless objects – summarily assembled on a board and coated in a brownish substance, a kind of *impasto* as solid as it is repugnant. Here, Miller engages in dialogue with Marxist theories on the *waste* of production, pushing the idea that the sphere of utility has of art to its logical extreme: an excremental tide. Seemingly at the aesthetic antipodes of Miller, Jeff Koons pursues comparable aims, but by systematically reversing the codes of value. Taking children's toys, cheap trinkets or department store packaging, Koons effaces their provenance by coating them with ostentatious codes of wealth: luxurious materials (chromed steel, porcelain), profuse ornamentation, impeccable finishes and monumental dimensions. If Koon's work proves seductive, this is because it stems from a world where waste seems inconceivable – where sumptuousness coats everything and surplus value is the golden rule of aesthetics: a standardized, rapid and efficient operation loudly transforming the slightest trifle into a gem. In this universe of intense lights, display windows, gift-boxes and advertising, nothing exists outside of the shopping mall. And if Koon's work proves fascinating and disconcerting despite the heavy-handed formal contrivances, this is because his imagery is consensual from the get-go. From Michael Jackson to stuffed animals, the object must be inoffensive and popular, while at the same time provoking a vague sense of emotional culpability. Koons exploits an intermediary zone between waste and popular culture, to which everyone seems tied by uneasy affections.

Gabriel Orozco lays hold of debris of another kind, unmediatized by commerce. It seems that a constant, centripetal motion animates his works. The artist occupies the centre, like a magnet drawing to itself the most shapeless of perishable matter. One of his earliest pieces, *My Hand is the Memory of Space* (1991), presents this image literally: a series of ice-cream cones spreads over the gallery floor, starting at the hollow imprint of the artist's hand. The economy of means Orozco employs is translated into gestures of *impression* (tattooing, brands, incisions or stamps applied to different media and materials) and set up by photographic *framing*. In the process, Orozco marks the forms he finds on the street or in nature – essentially ephemeral and fortuitous – as sculptures. More or less the entirety of his work derives from a vast array of waste, from animal fossils to demolition material; it includes stones, branches, industrial refuse (*Penske Work Project*, 1998) and, still more emblematically, lint from dryers (*Lintels*, 2001); all that remains is dust and fibre . . . *Pinched Stars* (1997) – a mass of shapeless and 'dripping' sculptures in aluminium on the ground – takes the question of art as an expelled object head-on. Orozco acknowledges that they seem 'clumsy or intricate, like a piece of shit. It's very scatological in the end.'[18] That said, the tension pervading his work opposes nature and culture in a world fashioned entirely by industry. His *oeuvre* draws a zone in escheat, urban and deserted at once, where human beings exist only through the prints they have left behind, signs of retreat – like ghosts wandering in a suburb the size of the globe. All that remains, then, are two poles that overlap without cease: data-processing and archaism. On the one hand, one finds fractal geometry, design software and complex materials such as polyurethane and synthetic polymer. On the other hand, there are cacti, bones, vegetable matter and ancestral practices involving terra cotta and graphite. Between the two stands the human being, at the mercy of both orders.

'On Some Motifs in Baudelaire', by Walter Benjamin, draws a parallel between work on the assembly line and games of chance, both of which must be taken up again

18   Quoted in Ann Temkin, *Gabriel Orozco* (New York: Museum of Modern Art, 2009), 130.

and again. The next morning, the previous day's efforts are gone, and the roulette wheel has stopped spinning; the gambler, like the labourer, has to start from scratch.

> The hand movement of the worker at the machine has no connection with the preceding gesture for the very reason that it repeats that gesture exactly . . . Each operation at the machine is just as screened off from the preceding operation as a *coup* in a game of chance is from the one that preceded it.[19]

As the negation of experience – that is, of what has been acquired, and therefore bare of all waste – the lottery of our times excludes unprofitable accumulation *a priori*. A universe from which all waste has been definitively evacuated, relegated to an obscure underground, and made forever invisible and *subsidiarized* (*filialisé*): this is the repression underlying the phantasmagoria of the age. On the one hand, it amounts to a world without remainder – arranged as a factory for living, incessantly 'cleaned' by design. On the other, it is riddled with emissions, *favelas* and suburbs; obsessively, it pushes the nomadic, the migrant, the filthy and the obsolete outside the city gates. It is only right to be scandalized by such a list, which lumps together human beings and objects; that said, what distinguishes the contemporary register of downgrading (*déclassement*) is that it does not bother with details.

Precisely here, the age-old tension between art and labour resurfaces, but on a different level than in modernism. In contrast to the latter, contemporary art does not deny the existence of waste as such: now, nothing and no

19   Benjamin, *Illuminations*, 177.

one can be deemed non-integrable. The vigour of the work of art stems from participating in both categories, circulating freely between the universe of products and the world of waste, simultaneously constituting a remainder and a value; it exploits its sociocultural utility and its dysfunctional quality by turns. Art's social function involves reconciling these two worlds by giving them a meaning. And if art gives rise to so many controversies, it is because this social function provides the object of a precarious consensus – one up for grabs again and again.

Today, filmmakers, artists and writers depict a world invaded by filth, corroded by social precarity, crowded with industrial objects designed for obsolescence, and saturated with ephemeral information. A popular image occurs in *WALL-E*, the Pixar Studios film about a robot busy cleaning a planet Earth filled with the detritus its erstwhile inhabitants have left behind. The contemporary cultural archive teems with proliferating and burdensome matter. Museum holdings are problematic: the mass of art objects produced every year defies anyone and everyone's capacity for memorization or judgement. As such, the question of waste – and the principles governing its elimination – will be posed in two ways in the future: in terms of centrifugal movement, which concerns apparatuses of power, and in terms of the centripetal dynamic animating countervailing artistic forces.

Modern art brought attention to bear on objects excluded by the dominant idealism. Georges Bataille shed light on the repulsive *remainder* left behind by the Hegelian totality; Walter Benjamin explored tiny pieces of debris from collapsed social edifices; Louis Althusser valorized aleatory surges of history; cultural studies focused on products and productions left over by the dominant culture. The analysand and the madman, the proletarian and the undocumented worker, labourers breaking stones, and ordinary people – all found a place in this counter-narrative, this great movement seeking to bring those expelled by ideology, deported from symbolic power, back to the centre of life and culture. From Courbet to Orozco, a realist mode of conceiving art has refused the existence of the inassimilable and waste, contested the division performed by ideological state apparatuses, and promoted a nominalist vision in which the singular, the exception, reigns.

And so we have arrived at a moment where the *après-coup* finally dominates the historical moment. Waste, what the process of production leaves behind, has assumed a preponderant position in politics, economy and culture. Today, the writing of History and psychoanalysis meet up, via this notion of *belatedness*, in the field of art. The past is not only reactivated by the present; the very nature of 'necessity' (which is supposed to direct it) depends on the vagaries of the present. The work of art offers not just formal content, but corresponding interpretive and historical contexts. It practises genealogy. It remains to be seen how the artists and thinkers of our times will respond to this open question, and according to what criteria 'historical rescue' will occur; henceforth, it is no longer the prerogative of the materialist historian, but the business of all.

Index

Printed in the United States
by Baker & Taylor Publisher Services